The Essential Confucius

Other HarperSanFrancisco Books
by Thomas Cleary

The Secret of the Golden Flower
The Essential Tao
The Essential Koran

THE ESSENTIAL
CONFUCIUS

The Heart of Confucius' Teachings
in Authentic *I Ching* Order

A Compendium of Ethical Wisdom

translated and presented by
Thomas Cleary

 HarperSanFrancisco
A Division of HarperCollinsPublishers

THE ESSENTIAL CONFUCIUS: *The Heart of Confucius' Teachings in Authentic I Ching Order.* Copyright © 1992 by Thomas Cleary. All rights reserved. Printed in the United States of America. No part of this book may be used or reproduced in any manner whatsoever without written permission except in the case of brief quotations embodied in critical articles and reviews. For information address HarperCollins Publishers, 10 East 53rd Street, New York, NY 10022.

FIRST HARPERCOLLINS PAPERBACK EDITION PUBLISHED IN 1993
ISBN 0–06–250215–8 (pbk)

An Earlier Edition of This Book Was Cataloged as Follows:
 Confucius
 [Lun yü. English]
 The essential Confucius: the heart of Confucius' teachings in authentic I ching order / Thomas Cleary. — 1st ed.
  p. cm.
 Translation of: Lun yü.
 Includes bibliographical references.
 ISBN 0–06–250157–7 (cloth)
 I. Cleary Thomas F., 1949–   . II. Title.
 PL2478.L3   1991   91–55282
 181'.09512—dc20   CIP

93 94 95 96 97 RRD(H) 10 9 8 7 6 5 4 3 2 1

This edition is printed on acid-free paper that meets the American National Standards Institute Z39.48 Standard.

CONTENTS

ACKNOWLEDGMENTS

Many people have contributed to the publication of this work, which is a result of more than two decades of research. Thanks are due to E. Bruce Brooks, an inspiring teacher who introduced me and many other students at Harvard to the subtleties of the original Confucius over twenty years ago. Thanks are also due to Wang Ailan, Lin I-kuan, and Lin Jin-duan, for countless demonstrations of Confucian virtues in the course of many years of acquaintance. For the method of constructing abstract systems from the *Book of Change* (popularly known under its Chinese title as the *I Ching*), I am indebted to the work of Liu I-ming. For assistance with practical experiments in analytic use of the *Book of Change,* thanks are due to Hope Hopper. Thanks are also due to Shambhala Publications, Inc., 300 Massachusetts Avenue, Boston, Massachusetts, for permission to reprint *Book of Change* aphorisms from *I Ching Mandalas,* translated by Thomas Cleary, © 1989. For assistance with preparation of the manuscript, thanks are due to Katherine Garcia. For seeing to the publication of the work, thanks are due to Pamela Pasti, literary agent, John Loudon, senior editor at Harper San Francisco, and other members of the Harper staff.

Confucius is one of the great figures in the history of human thought, a pioneering educator, social critic, and political scientist. As a philosopher and teacher, Confucius addressed core human issues with an aptitude for which his sayings have been preserved and studied over thousands of years. The collection known as the *Analects,* or aphorisms of Confucius, is among the most influential books in history, a basic sourcebook for a wide range of advice on human affairs, from governing nations and managing enterprises, to dealing with society and getting along with friends, to maintaining the family and mastering oneself.

Today the name of Confucius is better known than what he taught, yet his views on personality, social relations, and the human condition are ever more incisive as history intensifies the gravity of the very concerns he voiced twenty-five centuries ago. As one of the early critics of aggression, dictatorship, and militarism, Confucius speaks to a deeply felt longing for human dignity and social justice that may be found among people of conscience through the ages.

Like other great thinkers of the East, Confucius was not a dogmatic preceptor, and his essential teachings are generally broad enough to have borne reinterpretation through the ages as different cultures and societies periodically updated their understanding of his message to apply to the realities of their own times.

A major obstacle to absorbing the ideas of Confucius is the unsystematic arrangement of the *Analects.* The ancient Chinese would learn the whole collection by memory. Because they were dealing with aphoristic material, and doing so in a manner that required individualized study, they may not have cared very much about the order in which the sayings were written down. But this feature of the book poses a problem to the efficiency-oriented Western mind operating within a more restricted pattern of time.

The aim of this presentation of the teachings of Confucius has been to produce a streamlined version in a convenient format, centered on a translation that reads easily and yields meanings directly without distracting the reader unnecessarily by the interjection of Sinological complications. In this new presentation, sayings of Confucius from the *Analects* are arranged in small groups by topic, following his commentaries on imagery in the *I Ching,* or *Book of Change,* the most profound of the ancient Chinese classics that Confucius studied and promoted. These comments, which were incorporated into the *I Ching* itself, afford the most convenient lens through which to view the ideas of Confucius systematically.

Apart from the great advantage Confucian commentary in the *Book of Change* affords in the ease with which it can be used to elucidate the *Analects* of Confucius, it also helps bridge the cultural gap created by the general difficulty of access to the Chinese classics in the West. The *Book of Change* is the only one of the original Chinese classics that is well known in the West, and thus it affords the best available guide to the philosophical roots of Confucius.

Employing the *Book of Change* to analyze and study Confucius, one of history's most distinguished students of that classic, also helps to surmount yet another problem, which is the difficulty of access to the basic sayings of Confucius that has been caused by centuries of shifting conventions and controversies in later Confucian scholarship. Fortunately the primary sources themselves, the aphorisms of Confucius as found in the *Analects* and in the *Book of Change,* clarify each other so vividly that the reader may thereby enter into a direct relationship with the ideas of Confucius.

In this volume, the Confucian sayings on the *Book of Change* images are arrayed together to serve two functions: first, the conceptual outlines of the total system can be easily scanned as a guide to the overall scope and structure of the philosophy of Confucius; second, the aphorisms on the images serve as an index of topics under which relevant sayings from the *Analects* may be found, making it a simple matter to consult Confucius readily on specific subjects.

1. The Philosophy of Confucius

Confucius worked for the revitalization of culture in its role as a means of cultivating human feelings and maintaining the integrity and well-being of a people. He envisioned a social order guided by reasonable, humane, and just sensibilities, not by the passions of individuals arbitrarily empowered by hereditary status, and warned of the social consequences if men in positions of power considered personal profit and advantage over public humanity and justice. Confucius believed in the regeneration of public and private conscience through education and the influence of unifying cultural ideals.

Confucius believed that the conduct of the affairs of a nation would benefit from maximum participation in government by cultivated people whose intellects and emotions had been developed and matured by conscious culture. As an educator, he helped people study a variety of subjects such as history, political science, sociology, literature, music, etiquette, and philosophy to deepen the human understanding. This study, he believed, could help people prepare themselves to take on deliberate social responsibility.

For those who were born into social prominence, Confucius regarded this sort of cultivation as a basic personal duty, insofar as their status had suprapersonal implications. For others, he saw personal development as a way to individual fulfillment that would also enable one to take an active role in the development of the community or society at large. In either case, the overall role of education was the general enhancement of the individual and of the succession of groups—family, community, nation—to which the individual actively belonged.

Confucius advocated the restoration of just government and the revivification of society through the cultivation of what he called the ideal cultured person, the exemplary individual. The word Confucius used to express this ideal was a class term that formerly meant scion of the ruling class, but he subtly transformed it into an abstract moral ideal, a quality of character. Because he thought that the rule of personal example was the most effective, Confucius believed the virtues of the exemplary individual should especially be cultivated by the ruling class.

The Confucian aphorisms on the major images of the *Book of Change* are particularly clear examples of the confluence of these themes, which ultimately lead to the idea of social order as the autonomous self-rule of the conscientious individual, with rulership a purely ceremonial function, that of presiding over formal invocations of the unity of the people.

In the perception of Confucius the qualities of the exemplary individual were to be found in any humane person, not only, and indeed not necessarily, in hereditary aristocrats. The potential for this development was no longer considered a privilege inherited by certain families but a human endowment that was at once natural and divine and should be socially supported on an egalitarian basis. Confucius said, "Where there is education, there are no classes."

Confucius accordingly endeavored to make the tools for this development more available by passing on the heritage of history and culture to a wider range of people than would otherwise have had access to it. At the same time, he called upon people in positions of authority to make conscious human development part of the overall operation of society itself, not only in public education but in the actual operation of government, both for the general improvement of the mores of the people and for the cultivation of outstanding individuals with leadership qualities.

Confucius believed the moral foundation of social order must rest on the primary virtue of humaneness or humanity. Although the term is used dozens of times in the sayings of Confucius, rarely does the teacher approach a well-defined explanation of this virtue. Perhaps the simplest definition Confucius gives is that humanity is to love people; but then he does not define what he means by love. His reticence would seem to indicate the depth of Confucius' idea of humanity, of the respect with which he approached the question of what it meant to be humane and to love people, and also of the need he recognized for each individual to contemplate and approach humaneness in personal experience.

Confucius expected people to do their own thinking and tried to stimulate them: he emphatically said he would not do people's thinking for them. Though he is therefore often very general and abstract, for that very reason there are many suggestions in the sayings of Confucius that can be thought-provoking in a wide range of contexts.

For example, addressing the question of what it means to be humane, in the sense of the quality of humanity as it should be, or the meaning of being human, in one statement Confucius speaks entirely in social terms: being respectful at home, serious at work, and faithful in human relations. How these qualities would be actualized would naturally depend on the culture in which they are being practiced, but the virtues themselves could hardly be considered culture-bound.

Ultimately the abstract virtue of humanity must be universally adaptable if it is to be relevant to the many ways in which the human condition can evolve. To fulfill one's humanity, it is necessary to understand how to express humaneness usefully; thus Confucius also says, "How can one be humane without knowledge?" Elsewhere Confucius enumerates five practices characteristic of humanity that operate in the social sphere yet are defined by the teacher in terms sufficiently abstract to be universalized: respectfulness, magnanimity, truthfulness, acuity, and generosity.

Confucius also includes social action and self-improvement in the practice of humanity: "As for the humane, while they want to be established themselves, they establish others. While they want to succeed themselves, they help others to succeed. They can draw lessons from nearby. These can be called methods of humaneness." Confucius believed that if enough people behaved in such a manner, then the problems of society would gradually become manageable. But Confucius did not believe in miracles; he maintained that it would still take a century of good government to attain a normalization of humanity.

Next to humanity, Confucius seems to emphasize the virtue of justice. This word can also be translated "duty," or "principle"; the meanings of *justice, principle,* and *duty* should be understood to be intimately related in the original thought of Confucius. One of his most famous sayings contrasts the exemplary individual with the small-minded person in terms of whether one is informed by justice and duty or by profit and advantage.

Confucius thought that rulers who put on a pretense of justice and duty but were really motivated by profit and advantage were destroying the moral fiber of society. Therefore, because later usage tinged *duty* with notions of unquestioning obedience to superior authority, including the superior authority of convention, use of the word *duty* to translate the idea Confucius intended here creates some problems. This concept of duty lends itself to usurpation by established powers as a supposed moral underpinning for dictatorship and despotism.

Dictatorship and despotism were precisely what Confucius opposed; his idea of duty was obligation to justice, not to personalities empowered by hereditary authority. That this characterization of the teacher's concept of duty is truthful and not an invention of later Neo-Confucian idealists may be suggested to the thoughtful by considering how easily such an intelligent and educated man might have spent all his life in the employ of virtually any noble or lord he wanted to flatter or otherwise deceive. The life that Confucius actually led is probably the best evidence that his sense of duty was based on an impersonal principle of justice: never well-to-do, he eked out a living as a teacher, and at an age when most men would be looking forward to retirement, he left the comfort of his home and family to spend fourteen years trying to bring about a revival of culture throughout China.

Somewhat subordinate to humanity and justice, but nevertheless occupying a central position in the moral outlook of Confucius, was the virtue of etiquette. In the society and thinking of Confucius, the meaning of etiquette included concepts of mannerly behavior in day-to-day life, proper enactment of social rituals like marriage and mourning, and protocols for international relations and official occasions. As a vehicle of individual and of collective emotional expression, etiquette is part of the very fabric of the social order, and Confucius approached the subject with corresponding gravity.

Confucius considered deference the basis of all etiquette. He regarded courtesy as an indication of the moral strength of a nation for what it showed of their mutual respect and mutual consideration, virtues that fortify a people. Thus his teaching on etiquette was not simply on the formalities of classical rites but on the function and spirit of courtesy and ritual: "If people cannot run a country by ritual and deference, what is ritual for?" and "If people are not humane, what is the use of ritual?"

Confucius also emphasized the need for knowledge, as evidenced in his lifelong commitment to education and mental development. The purpose of the knowledge he taught, however, was not fulfilled by intellectual exercise alone, but in the functional application of knowledge to the cultivation of the virtues of humanity, justice, and courtesy. Asked what he meant by knowledge, Confucius called it "knowing people," placing it in the context of his field of concern, seeking to understand human character and the results of individual and collective behavior in private and public life. In its highest development, knowledge was to become wisdom, able to comprehend particulars through a unified insight.

The glue that binds everything together in the pragmatic moral universe of Confucius is the virtue of truthfulness or trustworthiness, faithfulness to the ideals exemplified by the sum of the cardinal virtues of humanity, justice, courtesy, and wisdom. Confucius likened trust to the link between a vehicle and its source of power and taught that trust was absolutely essential to the life of a nation.

The political and intellectual leaders of a society were by definition holders of a trust, Confucius believed, and would ultimately be trusted by the people to the extent that they were truthful and faithful to their trust. In the same way, Confucius taught that each individual is the holder of a trust, the faculties and potential of humanity, to which there exists by nature a duty, but also a choice, to be truthful and faithful by virtue of the qualities of humaneness, justice, courtesy, and wisdom.

2. Historical Background of the Teachings of Confucius

Confucius did not consider himself the author of what he taught but rather an heir and transmitter of ancient learning developed over the course of many centuries. In order to understand the sense of mission that inspired Confucius, therefore, it is necessary to view it against the mythological and historical background of his own beliefs.

According to the worldview of Confucius, the culture he wanted to revitalize was epitomized in the enlightened reigns of several illustrious leaders of ancient times, dating as far back as the twenty-fourth century B.C., nearly two thousand years before his own time. The first three of these leaders, Yao, Shun, and Yü, are legendary representatives of government by virtue.

Yao and Shun were believed to have been so charismatic that they maintained order in the land simply by sitting in majestic repose facing the south; Yü labored for twelve years on waterworks to save the central plain of China from a great prehistoric flood. It was also in the age of Yao, Shun, and Yü that accession to the throne was accomplished for the last time without recourse to violence or hereditary privilege.

The last-mentioned Yü is regarded in traditional Chinese history as the founder of the first hereditary dynasty, the Xia (Hsia), which was to last for more than four hundred years, from 2197 to 1766 B.C. Archaeologists have not yet found reliable evidence of the historicity of the Xia, but the archaeological record is in any event scanty for such ancient times.

According to traditional history, the last ruler of the Xia dynasty was in power for fifty-three years and became an oppressive tyrant. He was ultimately overthrown by the lord of one of the states of the confederation under Hsia leadership. The new king founded the Shang dynasty, later also called the Yin dynasty, which would last over six hundred years, from 1766 to 1100 B.C.

Modern archaeologists are satisfied as to the historicity of the Shang dynasty through the discovery of implements and writings from those times. Based on his own research, Confucius said the culture of the Shang/Yin followed on the Xia, and the sophistication of its art and writing would seem to argue for the actual existence of a well-developed precursor, even if no material remnants of that earlier civilization have been identified.

The confederations of tribes or states under the ancient dynasties seem to have been fairly loose, with considerable variety in local customs, so several systems of notation probably developed during the Yin dynasty. The earliest historical Taoist writing is attributed to the mentor and prime minister of the founder of that dynasty. It is claimed that the ancestors of Confucius were nobles in those times, and that would explain his access to traditions and tools of learning even six hundred years after the demise of the Yin dynasty.

The Yin dynasty was overthrown around 1100 B.C. by the house of Zhou (Chou), which rose to prominence under the leadership of King Wen and his sons King Wu and the Duke of Zhou. These three individuals are all heroes of Confucian tradition. King Wen won the support of other lords disaffected with the house of Yin, then ruled by an alcoholic psychopath. Perceived as a threat to the established order, King Wen was imprisoned. His son King Wu waged war against the ruler of the Yin dynasty and destroyed his power. King Wu and his brother the Duke of Zhou then established the Zhou dynasty, which was to last for many centuries.

King Wen and King Wu are revered not only as founders of the highly cultured Zhou dynasty but also as authors of the classic *Book of Change.* According to tradition, King Wen composed or compiled the core text during his imprisonment, and King Wu later elaborated it with more detailed analysis. King Wen apparently wrote the *Book of Change* as a guide to strategy and statecraft, but as a political prisoner he evidently found it expedient to maintain the antique format of oracular folklore and conceal the internal order of the work.

Deterioration in the Zhou dynasty became evident in the reign of the tenth king, during the ninth century B.C. For the first time a special bureau of investigation was established to ferret out critics of the government and execute them. The reign of the twelfth king, in the eighth century B.C., was also marked by oppression and violence. The house of Zhou split, and internal unrest was compounded by foreign invasion from the west.

The capital of the Chinese confederation was moved farther east in 770 B.C., beginning what is known as the era of the Eastern Zhou. By this time the political and cultural authority of Zhou as a unifying power was in serious decline, and competition among the various states of the confederation began to grow. In 685 B.C., the famous political philosopher Guan Zhong (Kuan Chung) became prime minister of the state of Qi (Ch'i), which rose to prominence in the confederation and temporarily became a stabilizing force through implementation of his policies.

Guan Zhong died in 642 B.C. The same year, Qi was attacked by another state. Hostilities soon began to break out among other states as well, and nine wars followed in the ninety years between the death of Guan Zhong and the birth of Confucius. Just ten years before Confucius was born, his native state of Lu established its first full-scale standing army. The father of Confucius was a soldier, who married late in life and died when Confucius was only two or three years old. His remote ancestors had been aristocrats in the state of Sung during the Shang/Yin dynasty many centuries earlier; the family had immigrated to the state of Lu because of assassinations, intrigue, and unrest in Sung.

Remote descendants of noble clans of antiquity formed a sector of society known as the *shi,* or knights, who were a kind of middle class between the ruling aristocracy and the peasantry, increasingly disenfranchised and impoverished. Many of the *shi* were military men, and Confucius himself is likely to have received some sort of martial training in his youth.

Growing up fatherless and poor, Confucius supported himself by working at various odd jobs, but he had set his heart on classical learning by the time he was fifteen years old. It was undoubtedly helpful to his studies that knowledge of archaic writing systems and ancient literature had been preserved in his home state of Lu, affording unusual opportunities for research into Chinese antiquities.

At the age of eighteen or nineteen, Confucius was married to a girl from his ancestral state of Sung, which was not very far from Lu. According to custom, his bride was probably fourteen or fifteen years old. They produced at least two children, a son and a daughter, and many people in China today claim to be their descendants.

Confucius began to work as a teacher when he was about twenty-three years old. By the time he was thirty, he had also served in the government of Lu, as a state granary manager of staple supplies and an overseer of public fields. During his twenties he also studied ancient government structures with a scholar known as the master of Tan, the lord of a small state who had joined the court of Lu.

In 517 B.C., when Confucius was in his middle thirties, a power struggle in Lu led to the emigration of the ruling lord duke to the state of Qi farther north. After this upheaval in the government of Lu, Confucius also went to Qi. Accounts differ as to the length of his stay there: one version of the story says that Confucius returned to Lu a year later; another has it that he remained in Qi for six or seven years. According to one account, Confucius became a retainer of a noble family of Qi, and he was also consulted by the lord duke of that state.

After Confucius returned to Lu, the government of his native state came under the control of one of its ministers. This strongman wanted to employ Confucius, but the scholar considered it unethical to work for usurped authority. Some years later the dictator was ousted by three powerful grandees, who subsequently employed Confucius in recognition of his refusal to work for the usurper. Over fifty years old by this time, Confucius was made first the governor of a city, then later the chief of the constabulary of Lu, a position of responsibility for the operation of justice. Not long afterward, his student Zilu was appointed administrator of the affairs of one of the powerful clans of Lu.

While Confucius was constabulary chief, he helped the lord duke Ding of Lu in successful negotiations with the ruler of Qi. He and Zilu also helped the latter's employers subdue certain retainers of powerful grandees who were trying to concentrate all the power they could into their own hands. After this period, things in Lu seemed to have become somewhat uncomfortable for Confucius, and in 479 B.C., then in his middle fifties, he set out on a journey that was to last fourteen years.

Over the course of these long and perilous travels, Confucius spent time in at least nine states of the old Zhou confederation, teaching students and seeking to spread his message of social regeneration among the holders of political power. The tide of the times was against him, however, as the competing states geared up for a protracted power struggle that was to reduce the China of the old Zhou order into a shambles over the following centuries.

Confucius returned to Lu in 484 B.C., nearly seventy years old. The same year, his son died, and two years later his greatest disciple Yan Hui also passed away. Confucius himself lived a while longer; he died in 479 B.C. at the age of seventy-three. The schools of his successors and heirs continued to operate privately through generations of turmoil and civil war, emerging publicly in peacetime hundreds of years later. The teachings of Confucius subsequently spread with the political and cultural influence of the Chinese empire, permeating civilization throughout East Asia with the spirit of respect for culture, education, and knowledge.

The Sayings

*Good people strengthen
themselves ceaselessly.*

Master Zeng, one of the pupils of Confucius, said, "I examine myself three times a day: have I been unfaithful in planning for others? Have I been unreliable in conversation with friends? Am I preaching what I haven't practiced myself?" (1:4)

Confucius said, "Don't worry about having no position; worry about that whereby you may effectively become established. Don't worry that no one recognizes you; seek to be worthy of recognition." (4:14)

Confucius said, "I have never seen anyone who was firm." Someone named a certain disciple. Confucius said, "He is covetous—how can he be firm?" (5:11)

A student said, "It is not that I do not like the teacher's way, but my strength is insufficient."

Confucius said, "Those whose strength is insufficient give up along the way; now you are drawing the line." (6:12)

Good people support others with enriched virtue.

Confucius said, "I still haven't seen anyone who likes humaneness and dislikes inhumanity. People who like humaneness couldn't be better, while those who dislike inhumanity are by that very fact practicing humaneness, because they are not allowing the inhumane to affect them. Are there any who can use their strength on humaneness for a whole day? I have never seen anyone who lacked the strength. There may be such people, but I have never seen any." (4:6)

Confucius said, "Only the humane can like people and can dislike people." (4:3)

A disciple asked Confucius about filial piety.
   Confucius said, "People who practice filiality today say they are providing a living, but even dogs and horses are taken care of; without respect, what is the difference?" (2:7)

Another disciple asked about filiality.
   Confucius said, "Expressions are difficult. If there is something to do, the younger sons take on the work. When there is wine and food, it is offered to the elders. Is this itself to be considered filial piety?" (2:8)

Good people order and arrange.

When Zihua, one of the disciples of Confucius, went on a mission to another state, another disciple, Zhanzi, asked for some grain for Zihua's mother. Confucius said to give her a certain amount. Zhanzi asked for more, and Confucius increased the measure. Still not satisfied, Zhanzi gave Zihua's mother even more than Confucius had indicated. Confucius said, "When Zihua went off, he was riding a well-fed horse and wearing light leather. I have heard that exemplary people help the needy and do not add to the wealth of the rich." (6:4)

The ruler of a certain state asked Confucius about government.

Confucius replied, "Have leaders be leaders, have administrators be administrators, have fathers be fathers, have sons be sons."

The ruler said, "Good! Of a truth, if leaders do not lead, administrators do not administer, fathers do not behave as fathers, and sons do not behave as sons, then even if there were grain, how could I eat of it?" (12:11)

*Good people nurture character
with fruitful action.*

A certain student was sleeping in the daytime.

Confucius said, "Rotten wood cannot be sculpted, a manure wall cannot be plastered. What admonition is there for me to give?" (5:10)

Confucius also said, "At first the way I dealt with people was to listen to their words and trust they would act on them. Now I listen to their words and observe whether they act on them. It was within my power to change this." (5:10)

Confucius said, "Good people should be slow to speak but quick to act." (4:24)

One of the disciples always used to say, "Neither harming nor importuning—how can this not be good?"

Confucius said, "How can this way be enough to be considered good?" (9:28)

Someone asked Confucius how to serve ghosts and spirits.

Confucius said, "As long as you are unable to serve people, how can you serve ghosts?"

The inquirer also asked about death.

Confucius said, "As long as you do not know life, how can you know death?" (11:12)

Confucius said, "To eat your fill but not apply your mind to anything all day is a problem. Are there no games to play? Even that would be smarter than doing nothing." (17:22)

A disciple asked Confucius, "Do cultivated people value courage?"

Confucius said, "Cultivated people consider justice foremost. When cultivated people have courage without justice, they become rebellious. When petty people have courage without justice, they become brigands." (17:23)

Good people enjoy life.

Confucius said, "The knowing enjoy water, the humane enjoy mountains. The knowing are diligent; the humane are quiet. The knowing are happy, the humane are long-lived." (6:23)

When at ease, Confucius was relaxed and genial. (7:4)

Confucius said, "Even if my fare is plain and my lifestyle austere, I still find pleasure in them. Riches and status unjustly attained are to me like floating clouds." (7:15)

An official of the state of Chu asked one of Confucius' disciples about the teacher, but the disciple didn't answer. Confucius remarked, "Why didn't you say, 'His character is such that he gets so enthusiastic that he forgets to eat, and is so happy that he forgets worries; he is not conscious of impending death'?" (7:18)

When they do things, good people plan first.

A certain elder statesman of Lu was said to act after reflecting three times. When Confucius heard of this, he said, "Reflecting twice will do." (5:20)

Confucius said, "People who do not think far enough ahead inevitably have worries near at hand." (15:12)

A disciple asked about exemplary people.
   Confucius said, "Apply their words before following them." (2:13)

Good people embrace the populace and nurture the masses.

When Confucius was in the state of Chu, he said, "Shall I go home? Shall I go home? The youth of my neighborhood are free-spirited and splendidly cultured; I don't know how their fine tuning will be accomplished." (5:22)

A disciple said, "If one can be generous to people and can help the masses, how would that be? Could it be called humaneness?"
 Confucius said, "One would not only be humane; one would surely be a sage. Even [the legendary wise kings] Yao and Shun had trouble doing this." (6:30)

Someone asked Confucius about humaneness.
 Confucius said, "When you are away from home, be as if meeting an important guest. When you employ people, be as if you were in charge of an important ceremony. What you do not like, do not pass on to others. Have no enmity in your land, no enmity at home." (12:2)

A disciple asked Confucius about humaneness.
 Confucius said, "Love people."
 Then the disciple asked about knowledge.
 Confucius said, "Know people."
 The disciple didn't understand.
 Confucius said, "Promote the honest, placing them over the crooked, and you can cause the crooked to straighten out." (12:22)

Confucius said, "If leaders are courteous, their people will not dare to be disrespectful. If leaders are just, people will not dare to be intractable. If leaders are trustworthy, people will not dare to be dishonest." (13:4)

Confucius remarked, "It is said that if good people work for a country for a hundred years, it is possible to overcome violence and eliminate killing. This saying is indeed true." (13:11)

Ancient kings set up myriad
realms and associated with their
representatives.

Confucius said, "If people have no faith, I don't know what they are good for. Can a vehicle travel without a link to a source of power?" (2:22)

Confucius said, "The way ideal people relate to the world is to avoid both rejection and attachment. To treat others justly is their way of association." (4:6)

Good people refine cultured qualities.

Confucius said to Zichan, a famous prime minister of the state of Zheng, "The way of exemplary people is fourfold. They are deferential in their own conduct, respectful in their service of employers, generous in taking care of people, and just in employing people." (5:16)

Confucius said, "When one has more substance than culture, one is a rustic; when one has more culture than substance, one is a literatus. Only when one has both substance and culture is one an exemplary person." (6:18)

Confucius went into the great national shrine and asked about everything. Someone remarked, "Who says that old man knows the classical rites? When he goes to the great shrine he asks about everything."
    Hearing of this, Confucius said, "This is part of the ritual." (3:15)

Confucius said, "In archery, the target is not the main thing, because of different grades of strength. This was the ancient way." (3:16)

Confucius was warm yet strict, stern but not fierce, respectful yet at ease. (7:37)

Confucius said, "To be respectful without manners is tiresome. To be circumspect without manners is timidity. To be brave without manners is wildness. To be straightforward without manners is strangling." (8:2)

Confucius said, "If you study culture widely and sum it up in an orderly way of life, you may thereby avoid being uncivilized." (12:15)

Someone asked Confucius about humaneness.
    Confucius replied, "Be respectful at home, serious at work, faithful in human relations. Even if you go to uncivilized areas, these virtues are not to be abandoned." (13:18)

*Good people distinguish above
and below and settle the ambitions
of the people.*

A pupil asked Confucius, "If one is poor but does not curry favor, or is rich but not haughty, how would that be?"

Confucius said, "Fine, but not as good as one who is poor but takes pleasure in the Way, or one who is rich but still courteous." (1:15)

Confucius said, "Exemplary people understand matters of justice; small people understand matters of profit." (1:16)

The ruler administers the way of heaven and earth and assists the proper balance of heaven and earth, thereby helping the people.

Confucius said, "Great indeed was the leadership of [the ancient sage-king] Yao! With magnificent grandeur, only Heaven is great, and only Yao emulated it. Such was their freedom that the people had no name for it. Magnificent was his achievement of works; brilliant was his establishment of culture." (8:19)

Confucius said, "I can find no flaw in [the ancient sage-king] Yü. He ate simply and paid respects to ghosts and spirits. He wore ragged clothes and beautified ceremonial garb. He lived in a humble dwelling, and exerted his strength on irrigation channels. I can find no flaw in Yü." (8:21)

A certain duke asked Confucius, "Is there a single saying by which it is possible to make a country thrive?"

Confucius replied, "Words cannot be like this, but they can come close. People say, 'It is hard to be a ruler, and not easy to be a minister.' If you know the difficulty of being a ruler, is this not close to a saying by which a country can be made to thrive?"

The duke asked, "Is there a single saying by which a country can be ruined?"

Confucius replied, "Words cannot be like this, but they can come close. People say, 'I take no pleasure in being a ruler; I only take pleasure in not being contradicted by others.' If you are good and no one contradicts you, isn't that also good? If you are not good but no one contradicts you, isn't that close to one saying that ruins a country?" (13:15)

A certain pupil asked Confucius about government: "What qualifies one to participate in government?"

Confucius said, "Honor five refinements, and get rid of four evils. Then you can participate in government."

The pupil asked, "What are the five refinements?"

Confucius said, "Good people are generous without being wasteful; they are hardworking without being resentful; they desire without being greedy; they are at ease without being haughty; they are dignified without being fierce."

The pupil asked, "What does it mean to be generous without being wasteful?"

Confucius replied, "To benefit the people based on what they find beneficial. Is this not generosity without waste?"

Confucius continued, "If they work hard after having chosen what they can work hard at, who would be resentful? If you want humaneness and get humaneness, then why would you be greedy? Cultivated people do not dare to be inconsiderate, whether of many or few, of the small or the great, of the young or the old; is this not ease without haughtiness? Cultivated people are proper in dress and solemn in mien, so that others are awed when they look at them; is this not dignity without ferocity?"

The pupil asked, "What are the four evils?"

Confucius replied, "To execute without having admonished; this is called cruelty. To examine accomplishments without having instructed; this is called brutality. To be lax in direction yet make deadlines; this is called viciousness. To be stingy in giving what is due to others; this is called being bureaucratic." (20:4)

Good people are parsimonious with power and avoid trouble; they are not susceptible to material inducements.

Confucius said, "Exemplary people concern themselves with virtue, small people concern themselves with territory. The ruling class thinks of punishment, the lower classes hope for benevolence." (4:11)

Confucius said, "It was magnificent the way [the ancient sage-kings] Shun and Yao held the world, and without getting involved in it." (8:18)

Confucius said, "It's hard to find anyone who has studied for a few years without seeking a grant." (8:12)

*Good people distinguish things in
terms of categories and groups.*

Confucius said, "Three kinds of friends are beneficial, and three are harmful. When friends are honest, sincere, or knowledgeable, they are beneficial. When friends are pretentious, fawning, or opportunistic, they are harmful." (15:37)

Confucius said, "Those whose paths are not the same do not consult one another." (15:40)

Confucius said, "Those who are born knowing are best; those who know by learning are next. Those who study only when they come to an impasse rank after that. Those who do not study even when at an impasse are considered lowest of the people." (16:9)

Confucius said, "Those who have virtue have something to say, but those who have something to say do not necessarily have virtue. Humanitarians are courageous, but the courageous are not necessarily humane." (14:5)

Confucius said, "There are cultivated people who are not humane, but there are no petty people who are humane." (14:7)

Good people stop evil and promote good, obeying Heaven and accepting its order.

Confucius said, "Wealth and rank are desired by people, but they do not stay if they are not gotten in the right way. Poverty and lowliness are disliked by people, but they do not leave if this is not accomplished in the right way. If exemplary people departed from humaneness, how could they be worthy of the name? Ideal people do not deviate from humaneness at any time; they are at it even when in a rush, they are at it even in the midst of turmoil." (4:5)

When Confucius saw the ill-reputed wife of a certain lord, one of his disciples expressed displeasure. Confucius said, "If I have done anything wrong, may Heaven reject it!" (6:28)

Good people decrease what is too much to add to what is too little, assessing things and dealing impartially.

Confucius said, "If you like humaneness but don't like learning, it degenerates into folly. If you like knowledge but don't like learning, it degenerates into looseness. If you like trust but don't like learning, it degenerates into depredation. If you like honesty but don't like learning, it degenerates into stricture. If you like bravery but don't like learning, it degenerates into disorder. If you like strength but don't like learning, it degenerates into wildness." (17:8)

Confucius remarked of a famous statesman who had lived nearly two centuries earlier, "He was a man of small capacity."

Someone said, "He was frugal, wasn't he?"

Confucius said, "He had three homes and families, and didn't take care of a whole range of official duties. How could he be considered frugal?"

The questioner said, "Then did he know about manners?"

Confucius said, "When the ruler of his state had a fence built around the palace, that statesman also had a fence built around his own mansion. When the ruler of his state met with other heads of state, a ceremonial wine stand was set up as a symbol of cordiality. That statesman also had such a ceremonial stand in his own house. If he knew about manners, who does not know about manners?" (3:22)

Someone said to Confucius, "If aggressiveness, conceit, enmity, and greed do not act in one, that can be considered humanity."

Confucius replied, "It can be considered difficult, but I don't know whether it is humanity." (14:2)

Ancient kings made music to honor virtue, offering it in abundance to God; thereby they shared it with their ancestors.

Confucius commented on two works of classical music: the *Shao*, or "The Accession," and the *Wu*, or "The Warrior." The former celebrates the peaceful enthronement of a sage-king in middle antiquity; the latter celebrates the overthrow of a tyrant by a just leader in late antiquity.

Confucius said, "'The Accession' is thoroughly beautiful and also thoroughly good. 'The Warrior' is thoroughly beautiful but not thoroughly good." (3:25)

When Confucius heard "The Accession" performed in the state of Qi, he did not know the taste of meat for three months. He said, "I had not expected that the performance of music could attain to this." (7:13)

Commenting on a classic song, Confucius said, "It is merry without being bawdy, melancholy without being painful." (3:20)

Speaking to the grand maestro of Lu about music, Confucius said, "Music is readily known. First the music rises, like a flock of birds; then this is followed by purification, clarification, continuation, and thus conclusion." (3:23)

*Good people go inside and rest
when the sun goes down.*

Confucius remarked, "I wish to say nothing."

One of his pupils said, "If you said nothing, what would the disciples have to pass on?"

Confucius retorted, "What does the sky say? The four seasons go on in it, all beings are born under it, but what does the sky say?" (17:19)

Confucius said to his foremost disciple, "To act when employed and hide when rejected—it seems only you and I can do this." (7:10)

Confucius said, "To pursue oddities only leads to harm." (2:16)

One of the disciples said, "It is possible to hear about the teacher's exoteric culture, but it is not possible to hear him speak of nature and the Way of Heaven." (5:13)

*Good people inspire others
and nurture virtue.*

Confucius said, "Cultivated people foster what is good in others, not what is bad. Petty people do the opposite." (12:16)

A grandee of Lu was troubled about thievery, and asked Confucius about it. Confucius said, "If you were not covetous, people wouldn't steal even if they were rewarded for it." (12:18)

Confucius said, "How dare I presume to sagehood, or even humaneness? It is just because I strive for them untiringly and teach people unwearyingly that something of that nature may be said." (7:33)

A disciple asked Confucius about humaneness.

Confucius said, "You are humane if you can practice five things in the world: respectfulness, magnanimity, truthfulness, acuity, and generosity. If you are respectful, you won't be despised. If you are magnanimous, you will win people. If you are truthful, you will be trusted. If you are acute, you will be successful. If you are generous, you will be able to employ people." (17:6)

Leaders draw on limitless resources of education and thought to embrace and protect the people without bound.

Confucius said to a pupil, "Do you think I have come to know many things by studying them?"

The pupil said, "Yes. Isn't it so?"

Confucius said, "No. I penetrate them by their underlying unity." (15:3)

Confucius said, "Study without thinking, and you are blind; think without studying, and you are in danger." (2:16)

Ancient kings set up education after examination of the region and observation of the people.

Confucius said of his foremost disciple, "I can talk to him all day, and he doesn't contradict me, as if he were ignorant. From what I observe of his private life after he has gone home, however, I find he has the ability to apply what he's learned. He is no ignoramus." (2:9)

Confucius said, "See what they do, observe the how and why, and examine their basic premises. How can people hide? How can people hide?" (2:10)

Confucius said, "I do not teach the uninspired or enlighten the complacent. When I bring out one corner to show people, if they do not come back with the other three, I do not repeat." (7:8)

Confucius said, "It is all right to talk of higher things to those who are at least middling, but not to those who are less than middling." (6:21)

Confucius said, "Enliven the ancient and also know what is new; then you can be a teacher." (2:11)

Confucius said, "If you don't talk with those worth talking to, you lose people. If you talk with those not worth talking to, you lose words. Knowers do not lose people, and they do not lose words either." (15:8)

*Ancient kings clarified penalties
and proclaimed laws.*

Confucius said, "If you love people, can you let them not work? If you are loyal to them, can you refrain from admonishing them?" (14:8)

Confucius said, "If you are personally upright, things get done without any orders being given. If you are not personally upright, no one will obey even if you do give orders." (13:6)

Good people clarify governmental affairs without presumptuous adjudication.

Someone said to Confucius, "Why don't you participate in politics?"

Confucius replied, "In a classic document it says, 'Filiality means friendship to siblings.' When this is applied to government, this is also participating in politics." (2:21)

Confucius said, "If one is not in such a position, one does not plan the policies." (8:14)

One of the elder statesmen of Lu asked Confucius, "How would it be to make the people serious and loyal, and thus enthusiastic?"

Confucius said, "Preside over them with dignity, and they will be serious. Be filial and kind, and they will be loyal. Promote the good, instruct the unskilled, and they will be enthusiastic." (2:20)

A disciple asked Confucius about government.

Confucius said, "Dwell on it tirelessly; carry it out faithfully." (12:14)

The administrator of a certain clan asked Confucius about government.

Confucius said, "Put the officers ahead of yourself, and forgive small errors. Appoint the wise and talented to office."

The administrator said, "How can I know the wise and talented to appoint them to office?"

Confucius said, "Appoint those you know of. As for those you don't know, will others ignore them?" (13:2)

*Those above secure their homes
by kindness to those below.*

When Confucius was an official of Lu, one of his disciples served as his steward. Confucius gave him nine hundred measures of grain, but the disciple refused.

Confucius said, "Don't refuse. Why not give it to your neighbors?" (6:5)

Confucius taught four things: culture, conduct, loyalty, and faith. (7:24)

Confucius fished with a pole, and did not use a net; when he hunted, he did not shoot roosting birds. (7:26)

Ancient kings shut the gates on the winter solstice: caravans did not travel, the ruler did not inspect the provinces.

Someone asked Confucius about shame.

Confucius said, "If you would be employed by a just country, it is shameful to be employed by an unjust country." (14:1)

Confucius said, "Cultivated people seek from themselves; small people seek from others." (15:17)

Confucius said, "Clever talk disrupts virtue; a little lack of forbearance disrupts great plans." (15:27)

Ancient kings promoted growth appropriate to the time and nurtured myriad beings.

A disciple asked Confucius, "If one can be generous to people and can help the masses, how is that? Could it be called humaneness?"

Confucius said, "Someone like that would not only be humane but would surely be a sage. Even [the legendary wise kings] Yao and Shun had trouble doing this.

"As for the humane, while they want to be established themselves, they establish others. While they want to succeed themselves, they help others to succeed. They can draw lessons from nearby. These can be called methods of humaneness." (6:30)

A pupil asked Confucius about government.

Confucius replied, "Lead them and work for them."

The pupil asked for more.

Confucius said, "Don't weary." (13:1)

When Confucius went to the state of Wei, he said to a disciple, "How the population has grown!"

The disciple asked, "Since they have a large population, what is there to add?"

Confucius said, "Enrich them."

The disciple asked, "Once they are rich, what else is there to add?"

Confucius said, "Educate them." (13:9)

Good people become acquainted with many precedents of speech and action in order to accumulate virtue.

Confucius said, "I was not born knowing anything; I was fond of the ancient and sought it keenly." (7:19)

Confucius said, "Give me a few more years, so that I will have studied the *Book of Change* for fifty years, and I may thereby eliminate major errors." (7:16)

Confucius said, "There are those who act without knowing; I will have none of this. To hear a lot, choose the good, and follow it, to see a lot and learn to recognize it: this is next to knowledge." (7:27)

Confucius said, "The Zhou dynasty took its lessons from the Xia and Yin [dynasties preceding it], resulting in a highly civilized culture. I follow Zhou." (3:15)

Good people are careful about what they say and moderate in eating and drinking.

Confucius did not talk about strange things, powers, chaos, or the spiritual. (7:20)

Confucius rarely spoke of profit, fate, or humaneness. (9:1)

Someone asked about humaneness. Confucius said, "The humane are restrained in their speech."

The inquirer asked, "Is that all there is to humaneness, being restrained in speech?"

Confucius replied, "When something is hard to do, can one not be restrained in speaking of it?" (12:4)

Confucius said, "Cultured people do not seek to eat to their fill or to live in comfort. They are keen in their work and careful about their words. They associate with those who have the Way, and are rightly guided by them. This can be called studiousness." (1:14)

Confucius said, "To be extravagant is presumptuous; to be frugal is stiffness. It is better to be stiff than presumptuous." (7:35)

Good people can stand alone without fear and can leave society without distress.

Confucius said, "An ideal person is not a tool." (2:12)

Confucius said, "A man who aspires to the Way yet is ashamed of poor clothing and poor food is not worth talking to." (4:9)

Praising a certain disciple, Confucius said, "His clothes are ragged, yet he is not embarrassed to stand alongside people wearing leather and fur." (9:27)

Confucius said, "To propitiate a spirit not one's own is to curry favor. To see justice but not do it is to lack courage." (2:24)

Confucius said, "Heaven gave birth to virtue in me; what can opponents do to me?" (7:22)

A disciple asked Confucius about clarity.
    Confucius said, "When biting and painful slander does not affect you, then you can be called clear. When biting and painful slander does not affect you, then you can be called perceptive." (12:6)

*Good people consistently practice
virtue and learn how to teach.*

Confucius said, "When you do things for your parents, admonish them gently. If you see that they are determined not to go along, then respect them and do not oppose them; and do not resent them for the trouble you've taken." (4:18)

Confucius said, "When the ancients did not speak out, it was because they were ashamed to say what they could not live up to themselves." (4:22)

Confucius said, "It is no problem for me to discern silently, to study tirelessly, and to teach indefatigably." (7:2)

Confucius said, "Aspire to the Way, rest on virtue, rely on humaneness, sport in the arts." (7:6)

Confucius said, "I can do nothing for those who do not ask themselves what to do." (15:16)

*Great people illumine the four
quarters with continuing light.*

A state border official asked to see Confucius. Confucius said, "I have never refused to see any worthy individual who has come here." So Confucius' assistant sent the official in to see the teacher.

When he came out, the official said to the disciples, "Why do you worry about being disenfranchised? The world has been unprincipled for a long time now. Heaven is going to make the teacher a cultural leader." (3:24)

*Good people accept others
with openness.*

Confucius said, "If the leaders are courteous, then the people are easy to employ." (14:43)

Confucius said, "If you are exacting with yourself but forgiving to others, then you will put enmity at a distance." (15:15)

*Good people stand without
changing places.*

Confucius said, "Observe a man's aspirations while his father is still alive; observe his actions after his father passes away. If he does not change his father's way for three years, then he can be called filial." (1:11)

Confucius said, "Hear the Way in the morning, and it would be all right to die that evening." (4:8)

Confucius said, "I haven't gotten to meet a sage, but if I get to meet an exemplary person, that will do. I haven't gotten to meet a good person, but if I get to meet someone who is constant, that will do. Those who pretend to have what they lack, who pretend to fullness when they are empty, can hardly be constant." (7:25)

Confucius said, "The armed forces may be deprived of their commander, but a man cannot be deprived of his will." (9:26)

Good people keep the petty at a distance, being stern without ill will.

Confucius said, "If you associate with those who are not centered in their actions, you will become either too uninhibited or too inhibited. Those who are too uninhibited are too aggressive, while those who are too inhibited are too passive." (13:21)

Confucius said, "Cultivated people are easy to work for but hard to please. If you try to please them in the wrong way, they are not pleased. When they employ people, they consider their capacities.

"Petty people are hard to work for but easy to please. Even if you please them by something that is wrong, they are still pleased. When they employ people, they expect everything." (13:25)

Confucius said, "Cultivated people are serene but not haughty. Petty people are haughty but not serene." (13:26)

Confucius said, "Clever talkers who put imperious expressions on their faces have little humaneness indeed." (1:3)

Confucius said, "I will have nothing to do with those who are free but not honest, childlike but not sincere, straightforward but not trustworthy." (8:16)

A disciple asked Confucius, "How is it when everyone in your hometown likes you?"
Confucius said, "Not good enough."
The disciple asked, "How about if everyone in your hometown dislikes you?"
Confucius said, "Not good enough. It is better when the good among the people like you and the bad dislike you." (13:24)

Confucius said, "A knight who is concerned about a dwelling place is not worthy of being considered a knight." (14:3)

Confucius said, "When I am with a group of people all day and the conversation never touches on matters of justice but inclines to the exercise of petty wit, I have a hard time." (15:17)

Good people refrain from
what is improper.

Confucius said, "If you act on the basis of profit, you will be much resented." (4:12)

Zigeng, one of the pupils of Confucius, said, "What I don't want others to do to me, I do not want to do to others." (5:12)

Confucius said, "I consider it shameful to be glib, to put on a commanding appearance, or to be fawning. I also consider it shameful to befriend someone while concealing a grudge." (5:25)

When one of his disciples was mayor of a certain city, Confucius said, "Have you found worthy people there?"

The disciple replied, "There is one who does not take shortcuts, and has never come to my office except on official business." (6:14)

Good people shine with the quality of enlightenment.

Confucius said, "Cultivated people are ashamed to say more than they can do." (14:29)

A disciple asked Confucius about the cultivated person.
Confucius said, "Cultivate yourself by seriousness."
The disciple asked, "Is that all?"
Confucius said, "Cultivate yourself to make others secure."
The disciple asked, "Is that all?"
Confucius said, "Cultivate yourself to make all people secure. Even the sage-kings had trouble cultivating themselves enough to make all people secure." (14:44)

Confucius said, "Even if you have fine abilities, if you are arrogant and stingy, the rest is not worth considering." (8:11)

*Good people deal with the
masses, acting unobtrusively while
in fact illumined.*

Confucius said of his foremost disciple, "He is wise indeed! He subsists on bare essentials and lives in a poor neighborhood; for other people this would mean intolerable anxiety, but he is consistently happy. Wise indeed is he!" (6:11)

Confucius said, "Don't worry about the recognition of others; worry about your own lack of ability." (14:32)

Confucius said, "Don't worry that other people don't know you; worry that you don't know other people." (1:16)

Confucius said to a disciple, "Shall I teach you how to know something? Realize you know it when you know it, and realize you don't know it when you don't." (2:17)

Confucius said, "Uncle Tai can be said to have been perfect in virtue. He conceded kingship three times, yet the people never found out or appreciated it." (8:1)

Confucius said, "A person can spread the Way, but the Way is not to aggrandize a person." (15:29)

Good people are factual in their speech, consistent in their deeds.

Confucius said to a disciple, "My way is permeated by unity!"

The disciple said, "Yes."

When Confucius had left, the students asked the disciple what the teacher had meant. He said, "The teacher's way is just being faithful and considerate." (4:15)

Confucius said of a certain man, "Who says he is honest? When someone asked him for some vinegar, he got some from a neighbor to give away." (5:24)

Someone said of a certain disciple, "He is a good man, but he is not a clever speaker."

Confucius said, "Why does he need to be a clever speaker? One who confronts people with an outpouring of verbiage is often disliked by others. Regardless of whether or not he is a good man, why should he need to be a clever speaker?" (5:5)

A disciple asked Confucius how to work for a ruler.

Confucius said, "Don't deceive him, even if you have to offend him." (14:23)

A noble man of ancient times was made a judge, but was removed from office three times. Someone said to him, "Don't you think it's time for you to leave?"

He replied, "If you serve people honestly, where can you go and not be ousted three times? If you work for people opportunistically, why leave your native place?" (18:2)

*Good people assimilate yet
are different.*

Confucius said, "Ideal people are universal and not clannish. Small-minded people are clannish and not universal." (2:14)

Confucius said, "When I do something in a group of three people, I always find my teacher there. I choose the good and follow it, and change what is not good." (7:21)

Confucius said, "Cultivated people harmonize without imitating. Immature people imitate without harmonizing." (13:23)

*Good people examine themselves
and cultivate virtue.*

Confucius said, "How I've deteriorated! It's been such a long time since I stopped seeing the Duke of Zhou in dreams." (7:5)

Confucius said, "Study as though you will not reach, as if you may lose it." (8:17)

Someone asked Confucius about cultivated people.
Confucius said, "Cultivated people are neither anxious nor fearful."
The inquirer retorted, "Is that all there is to being a cultivated person, to be 'neither anxious nor fearful'?"
Confucius said, "If one can examine oneself inwardly and find nothing blameworthy, what is there to worry about or to fear?" (12:4)

Confucius said, "The virtue of balanced normalcy is consummate, it seems, but it has been scarce among the people for a long time." (6:29)

Confucius said, "Determined people and humanitarians will not seek to live by means that would injure humanity, but they would kill themselves if that would perfect humanity." (15:9)

Confucius said, "Cultivated people have nine thoughts. When they look, they think of how to see clearly. When they listen, they think of how to hear keenly. In regard to their appearance, they think of how to be warm. In their demeanor, they think of how to be respectful. In their speech, they think of how to be truthful. In their work, they think of how to be serious. When in doubt, they think of how to pose questions. When angry, they think of trouble. When they see gain to be had, they think of justice." (16:10)

*Good people forgive faults and
pardon crimes.*

Confucius said, "People make mistakes according to their individual type. When you observe their errors, you can tell if people are humane." (4:7)

Confucius said of a disciple, "He is worthy of a wife. Even though he has been in prison, he wasn't at fault." Confucius married his daughter to him. (5:1)

Confucius said, "If they are directed by government policy and made orderly by punishment, the people will try to get off scot-free and feel no shame about it. If they are guided by charisma and unified by courtesy, they will be conscientious and upright of character." (2:3)

Confucius said of two famous purists, "They didn't think about past evils, so they were seldom resented." (5:23)

*Good people eliminate wrath
and cupidity.*

Confucius said, "If you can correct yourself, what trouble would you have in government? If you cannot correct yourself, what can you do about correcting others?" (13:13)

Confucius said, "To be poor without bitterness is easy; to be rich without arrogance is hard." (14:11)

Confucius said, "Can an ignoble man serve the government? No. He worries about getting something, and once he has got it he worries about losing it. As long as he worries about losing, there's no telling what he might do." (17:15)

Confucius said, "Exemplary people are even-tempered and clear-minded. Petty people are always fretting." (7:36)

*Good people better themselves
when they see a chance and correct
whatever faults they have.*

The ruler of Lu asked Confucius, "Who among your disciples is studious?"

Confucius replied, "There was one who was studious. He did not transfer anger and did not repeat a mistake. Unfortunately, he died young. Now that he is gone, I haven't heard of anyone who is studious." (6:3)

Confucius said, "If you make a mistake and do not correct it, this is called a mistake." (15:30)

Confucius said, "Is humaneness far away? If one wants to be humane, then humaneness is there." (7:29)

Confucius said, "Place loyalty and faithfulness first; don't associate with anyone who is not as good as you are, and don't hesitate to change when you have erred." (8:25)

A disciple asked Confucius about elevating virtue and clarifying confusion.

Confucius said, "To be guided by loyalty and faithfulness to what is right is to honor virtue. People wish for the life of those they love while wishing for the death of those they hate; once you wish for life, to also wish for death is confusion." (12:10)

Confucius said, "There are three things in the path of cultivated people of which I am incapable: the humane do not worry; the knowing are not confused; the brave are unafraid." (14:30)

Good people distribute blessings to reach those below them, while avoiding presumption of virtue.

Confucius said, "If people are in high positions but are not magnanimous, if they perform courtesies without respect, or if they attend
funerals without sadness, how can I see them?" (3:26)

Confucius said, "Virtue is never isolated; it always has neighbors."
(4:25)

Rulers announce their directives to the four quarters.

Confucius said, "To guide a state, be serious and faithful in its affairs; be economical and love the people, employing the citizens in season." (1:5)

Confucius said, "When government is done by virtue, it is like the North Star abiding in its position, with all the other stars surrounding it." (2:1)

A certain duke asked Confucius about government.

Confucius said, "If those nearby are pleased, those far away will come." (13:16)

Good people prepare weapons to guard against the unexpected.

Confucius said, "To go to war with untrained people is tantamount to abandoning them." (13:30)

Confucius said, "They are wise who do not anticipate deception and do not consider dishonesty, yet are aware of them from the start." (14:33)

Lord Ling of Wei asked Confucius about battle formations.

Confucius said, "I have heard something about the arrangement of ceremonial offerings, but I have never studied military affairs."

The next day Confucius left. (15:1)

Confucius said, "Few lose out on account of prudence." (4:23)

*Good people follow virtue, building
on the small to attain the great.*

Confucius said, "There are sprouts that do not send up shoots; there are shoots that do not bear fruit." (9:22)

A disciple asked Confucius about humaneness.

Confucius said, "To master oneself and return to courtesy is humaneness. If they would master themselves and return to courtesy, the whole world would take to humaneness. Do you think humaneness derives from oneself, or from others?"

The disciple asked for an outline.

Confucius said, "Do not regard what is not courteous. Do not listen to what is not courteous. Do not say what is not courteous. Do not do what is not courteous."

The disciple said, "I am not quick-witted, but I would like to work on these words." (12:1)

Confucius asked one of his disciples to compare himself to another, who happened to be the foremost of the students. The disciple said, "How could I dare even hope to be like him? When he learns one thing, he thereby knows ten; when I learn one thing, I only know two."

Confucius said, "You are not comparable to him. Neither am I, for that matter." (5:9)

A disciple asked Confucius about the way of good people.

Confucius said, "If you do not walk in their footsteps, you do not gain access to their abode." (11:20)

One of the disciples of Confucius who had become the administrator of a city asked the teacher about government.

Confucius said, "Don't wish for speed; don't see small advantages. If you wish for speed, you won't succeed; if you see small advantages, great things will not be accomplished." (13:17)

Confucius said, "No one knows me."

A disciple asked, "What do you mean, no one knows you?"

Confucius said, "I have no grudge against Heaven, nor do I blame other people. I study from the basis and arrive at higher things. Who knows me but Heaven?" (14:37)

Good people use life to the full and achieve their aim.

Once when two disciples were standing by Confucius, the teacher asked each one to express his ambition.

One disciple said, "I would like a carriage and clothes like those of my companions, and not to worry about them wearing out."

The other disciple said, "I would like to avoid taking pride in good and passing on toil to others."

One of the disciples then asked Confucius his wish. The teacher said, "To comfort the elderly, deal faithfully with friends, and care for the young." (5:26)

Confucius said of a certain disciple, "In a country with the Way he will not be a derelict, and in a country without the Way he will avoid getting executed." Confucius married his elder brother's daughter to him. (5:2)

Confucius said, "The knowing are not confused; the humane are not worried; the brave are not afraid." (9:30)

Confucius said, "Cultivated people reach upward; petty people reach downward." (14:24)

Confucius said, "Once I went all day without food and all night without sleep, just to think. It was no use. It's better to study." (15:31)

*Good people comfort others and
urge reciprocity.*

Confucius said, "It is beautiful to make humaneness one's home. If you do not choose to dwell in humaneness, how can you attain knowledge?" (4:1)

Speaking of a famous man known as "The Mediator," Confucius said, "'The Mediator' was skilled at social intercourse. Eventually people came to respect him." (5:17)

A disciple asked Confucius about government.

Confucius said, "See to it that there is enough food, enough arms, and the trust of the people in government."

The disciple asked, "If one of these unavoidably had to be omitted, which of the three would be first?"

Confucius said, "Omit arms."

The disciple asked, "If one of the remaining two unavoidably had to be omitted, which would go first?"

Confucius said, "Omit food. Since ancient times people have died, but nothing can be established without the trust of the people." (12:7)

Good people make calendars and clarify the seasons.

Confucius said, "Cultivated people have three disciplines. When they are young and their physical energy is not yet stabilized, they are disciplined in matters of sexuality. When they mature and their physical energy is at the peak of strength, they are disciplined in matters of contention. When they are old and their physical energy is in decline, they are disciplined in matters of gain." (16:7)

Good people stabilize life in the proper position.

Confucius said, "At the age of fifteen I set my heart on learning. At thirty I was established. At forty I was unwavering. At fifty I knew the order of Heaven. At sixty I listened receptively. At seventy I followed my heart's desire without going too far." (2:4)

One of the disciples was studying for employment.

Confucius said, "Learn a lot, eliminate the doubtful, and speak discreetly about the rest; then there will be little blame. See a lot, eliminate the perilous, act prudently on the rest; then there will be little regret. When your words are seldom blamed and your actions seldom regretted, employment will be there." (2:18)

Confucius said, "It is after the coldest weather that you know the pine and the cedar outlast the withering." (9:29)

*Good people cautiously practice
introspection.*

Confucius said, "As far as exterior culture goes, I guess I am comparable to others. When it comes to personal practice of an ideal life, I have not attained anything." (7:32)

Confucius eliminated four things: he had no willfulness, no insistence, no fixation, and no selfishness. (9:4)

Confucius said, "Is it all over? I still haven't found anyone who can see his faults and inwardly accuse himself." (5:27)

Once Confucius was going to have one of his disciples work for the government, but the disciple said, "I am not yet able to be sure about this." Confucius was pleased. (5:6)

Good people think without leaving their place.

Confucius said, "The people of the South have a saying that someone who has no constancy cannot be a shaman or a physician. This is a good saying. If you are not constant in your virtues, you may experience disgrace for it." (13:22)

Once on a journey Confucius and his followers were starving. His followers were so ill they couldn't get up. Irritated, one of the disciples went to see Confucius and said, "Can superior people also come to an impasse?"

Confucius replied, "Superior people can certainly come to an impasse. It is the petty person who loses self-control at an impasse." (15:2)

A disciple of Confucius was asked, "When the teacher comes to a state, he is always consulted about the government there. Does he seek this, or is it thrust upon him?"

The disciple said, "It happens because the teacher is warm, good, respectful, discreet, and deferential. It seems that the way the teacher seeks it is different from the way others seek it." (1:10)

Good people live wisely and improve customs.

Confucius said to a student, "Be an exemplary man of learning, not a trivial pedant." (6:13)

Confucius said, "Not cultivating virtue, not learning, not being able to take to justice on hearing it, and not being able to change what is not good: these are my worries." (7:3)

Confucius said, "Be dutiful at home, brotherly in public; be discreet and trustworthy, love all people, and draw near to humanity. If you have extra energy as you do that, then study literature." (1:7)

Good people persist to the end and find out if something is wrong.

ANALECTS

Confucius said, "If cultured people are not serious, they will not be dignified. When they learn, they are not inflexible. They place primary importance on loyalty and trustworthiness and do not befriend those who are not as good as they are. When they make mistakes, they do not hesitate to reform." (1:8)

Good people make judgments and execute punishments.

The ruler of the state of Lu asked Confucius, "What can be done to win the allegiance of the people?"

Confucius replied, "Promote the honest over the crooked, and the people will obey. Promote the crooked over the honest, and the people will not obey." (2:19)

Someone said to Confucius, "How would it be to respond to hostility with virtue?"

Confucius replied, "Then what would you use to respond to virtue? Respond to hostility with honesty; respond to virtue with virtue." (14:36)

Good people apply punishment with understanding and prudence and do not keep people imprisoned.

Confucius said, "Cultivated people make justice their sustenance, and carry it out in an orderly manner; they set it forth with humility, and actualize it by faithfulness." (15:18)

Confucius said, "Those who are not humane should not live in austerity for long, and should not live in comfort for long either. The humane rest in humaneness; those who know use humaneness advantageously." (4:2)

Good people articulate directions and carry out tasks.

The ruler of the state of Lu asked Confucius, "A ruler employs ministers; ministers work for the ruler: how should this be done?"

Confucius replied, "Let rulers employ their ministers courteously; let ministers work for their rulers loyally." (3:19)

A grandee of Lu asked Confucius about government.

Confucius replied, "Government means rectitude. If you lead correctly, who will dare not to be correct?" (4:17)

Confucius said, "Don't talk about what is already done; don't remonstrate about what is already over; don't criticize what has already happened." (3:21)

A disciple asked Confucius about effective action.

Confucius said, "If your words are truthful and your actions are in earnest, they will be effective even in foreign countries. If your words are not truthful and your actions not in earnest, do you think they would be effective even in your homeland? When you stand, see truthfulness and seriousness assembled before you; when you are in a carriage, see them leaning on the harness. After that you act effectively."

The disciple wrote this on his belt so that he would always remember. (15:6)

Good people form associations for education and action.

Confucius said, "At first the way I dealt with people was to listen to their words and trust they would act on them. Now I listen to their words and observe whether they act on them. It was within my power to change this." (5:10)

Confucius said, "When you see wise people, think of becoming equal to them. When you see unwise people, reflect inwardly on yourself." (4:17)

A pupil asked Confucius why a certain man was posthumously entitled "The Cultured One." Confucius said, "He was keen, fond of study, and not embarrassed to ask questions of his juniors. Therefore he is called cultured." (5:15)

Confucius said, "It may be possible to study together without being able to go on the way together. It may be possible to go on the way together without being able to take a stand together. It may be possible to take a stand together without being able to plan together." (9:31)

Confucius said, "Cultivated people are strict but do not contend; they associate with others but do not join factions." (15:27)

Ancient kings honored God and set up shrines.

Confucius said, "I can find no flaw in Yü [the enlightened founder of the ancient Xia dynasty]. He ate simply and paid respects to ghosts and spirits. He wore ragged clothes and beautified ceremonial garb. He lived in a humble dwelling, and exerted his strength on irrigation channels. I can find no flaw in Yü." (8:21)

Confucius said, "Suppose people could run a country by ritual and deference; there would be nothing to it. If people cannot run a country by ritual and deference, what is ritual for?" (4:13)

Confucius said, "If people are not humane, what is the use of rites? If people are not humane, what is the use of music?" (3:3)

Good people determine measures and discuss virtuous actions.

Someone asked Confucius how to elevate virtue, purge evil, and clarify confusion. Confucius said, "Good question! Put service first and gain after; is this not elevating virtue? Attack your own evils, not those of others; is this not purging evil? And suppose you forget yourself and affect your relatives because of a temporary fit of anger; is that not confusion?" (12:21)

A pupil asked about friendship. Confucius said, "Speak truthfully and guide them in good ways. If they do not agree, then stop and do not disgrace yourself for them." (12:23)

Good people consider judgments and postpone executions.

Confucius said, "To be bold and despise poverty leads to disorder. To hate people intensely for not being humane also leads to disorder." (8:10)

One of the grandees of the state of Lu was consulting Confucius about government: he said, "How would it be to kill those who lack the Way in order to take to those who have the Way?"

Confucius replied, "You are practicing government—what has that to do with killing? If you want goodness, the people will be good. The qualities of social leaders are wind, the qualities of the common people are grass; grass will always bend in the wind." (11:19)

*Good people are exceedingly
deferential in conduct, exceedingly
sad in mourning, exceedingly frugal
in consumption.*

Someone asked Confucius about the basis of ritual.

Confucius said, "This is a big question. In rites, frugality is preferable to ostentation. In funerals, sadness is more important than the arrangements." (3:4)

When Confucius ate beside someone in mourning, he never ate his fill. On a day that he had himself mourned, Confucius did not sing. (7:9)

Good people consider problems and prevent them.

One of the disciples of Confucius was offered a mayoralty by a corrupt aristocrat. The disciple said, "Decline tactfully for me. If anyone wants to bring me back, I'll be at the border." (6:5)

Confucius said, "Cultivated people do not contend over anything." (3:7)

A grandee of the state of Wei asked Confucius about the meaning of the proverb, "It is better to propitiate the hearth than the chamber."
Confucius said, "It is not so. Those who have offended Heaven haven't a prayer." (3:13)

Confucius said, "Study eagerly with earnest faith; keep to the good way even unto death. Do not enter a dangerous state; do not stay in a chaotic state. When the Way prevails in the world, appear in public life; when the Way does not prevail, disappear. When a country has the Way, it is a disgrace to be poor and lowly there. When a country lacks the Way, it is a disgrace to be rich and noble there." (8:13)

Confucius said, "In hearing complaints, I am like others; I would have it such that there be no complaints." (12:13)

Confucius said, "If a country is just, one speaks independently and acts independently. If a country is unjust, one acts independently but speaks conventionally." (14:4)

*Good people carefully discern things
and keep them in their places.*

One of the aristocrats of Lu asked Confucius if a certain disciple was humane. Confucius said he didn't know. The aristocrat kept asking, so Confucius finally said, "He could be employed to collect taxes for a fair-sized state, but I don't know if that means he is humane."

The aristocrat asked about another disciple. Confucius said, "He could be employed as the chief administrator of a large city or a powerful clan, but I don't know if that means he is humane."

Then the aristocrat asked about yet another disciple. Confucius said, "He could be dressed up as a courtier and employed to talk with guests, but I don't know if that means he is humane." (5:8)

A disciple asked Confucius about a certain prime minister of Chu who had lived a century earlier: "He became a prime minister three times, yet showed no joy on his face. He was deposed three times, yet showed no anger on his face, and always told the incoming minister about the affairs of government under the outgoing ministry. What would you say about him?"

Confucius said, "He was loyal."

The disciple asked, "Was he humane?"

Confucius said, "How can one be humane without knowledge?"

The disciple then asked Confucius about a man of the sixth century B.C. who abandoned his native state when a grandee killed the ruler. Coming to another state, he found affairs similar to those in his own, so he left that place too. A third state proved just as corrupt, and the man again left. The disciple wanted to know what Confucius would say about him.

Confucius said, "He was a purist."

The disciple said, "Was he humane?"

Confucius said, "How can one be humane without knowledge?" (5:19)

Speaking of a certain grandee of the state of Wei who had lived a century before his time, Confucius said, "When the country had the Way he would be knowledgeable; when the country lacked the Way he would be ignorant. His knowledge can be reached, but not his ignorance." (5:21)

Confucius said, "A cultivated person does not promote people on account of what they say, nor ignore what is said because of who is saying it." (15:23)

Confucius said, "When everyone dislikes something, it should be examined. When everyone likes something, it should be examined." (15:28)

NOTES

BOOK OF CHANGE 1

Although the Confucian view of humanity is essentially social, self-cultivation is also a primary responsibility of the individual to society, because ability to contribute to the well-being of society is greater or lesser in proportion to personal development. The *Great Learning,* another Confucian classic, says, "In ancient times, those who wished to illustrate the qualities of illumination throughout the world first brought order to their nations. Those who wished to bring order to their nations first balanced their families. Those who wished to balance their families first cultivated themselves. Those who wished to cultivate themselves first straightened their minds. Those who wished to straighten their minds first made their intentions sincere."

Analects 1:4

Master Zeng (Tseng) was forty-six years younger than the teacher, and therefore was a pupil of the mature Confucius. Master Zeng is one of the most important disciples of record, and some historians have assumed that he was one of those involved in the early collection and transmission of the *Analects,* being one of the few students referred to in this document as Master (*zi/tzu*), and the only one to be consistently so called. The *Classic of Filial Piety (Xiao jing/Hsiao Ching),* an important text in later Confucianism, has been attributed to the school of Master Zeng, even though the version known today was evidently written several centuries later.

Individual self-development is not just a means of personal improvement and fulfillment but at the same time a basis for enhancement of the family, the community, and society as a whole. A commitment to better oneself therefore implies dedication to the welfare of others.

Analects 2:7, 2:8

The disciples here are Ziyou (Tzu-yu) and Zixia (Tzu-hsia). Their names came to be synonymous with excellence in literary studies.

In 2:8, "Expressions are difficult," the reference is to the demeanor of younger people toward older people. The facial expression and other gestures and manners are considered an integral part of how people are treated. What is important is the whole interaction: not just the material fact of what is done for others, but also the mood and feeling that are conveyed. These things combine in the total social and psychological meaning of a relationship or an interaction.

BOOK OF CHANGE 3

Confucian thinking lays great emphasis on the value of order, the utilitarian worth of which came to be regarded as moral worth insofar as it deals in the elements of life and human welfare.

Analects 6:4

Zhanzi (Chan-tzu), or Master Zhan, was twenty-nine years younger than Confucius, one of the older of the most noted disciples. Master Zhan served as an administrator for a noble clan of the state of Lu.

Analects 12:11

The ruler was Duke Jing (Ching) of Qi (Ch'i), who appears several times in the *Analects*. Qi had become a very powerful state some time before Confucius, under the guidance of Guan Zhong (Kuan Chung), a distinguished philosopher-statesman. Guan Zhong belonged to a school of Legalism that incorporated Taoist elements of psychological training and strategy. Later beset by intrigue and mismanagement, Qi was eventually absorbed by Qin (Ch'in), a highly militarized state that was ultimately to take over all the ancient Chinese nation-states.

BOOK OF CHANGE 4

As in Buddhism and Taoism, in authentic Confucianism learning is not armchair philosophy; it must include praxis that empowers principles.

Analects 9:28

This disciple was Zilu (Tzu-lu), one of the noted students of Confucius. Zilu was particularly distinguished in political science.

Analects 11:12

This passage is frequently cited to illustrate the human basis of Confucian teaching in contrast to the more magical thinking of earlier dynasties.

Analects 17:23

The disciple here was again Zilu.

BOOK OF CHANGE 5

Confucius taught moderation and frugality, not asceticism. The culture he promoted was to function as a means of modulating and regulating the experience of life in such a way as to develop a balanced and rounded humanness.

Analects 7:18

The official here was Shen Zhuliang (Shen Chu-liang), duke of She, which was one of the prefectures of the state of Chu (Ch'u).

BOOK OF CHANGE 6

Strategy and planning form one of the major departments of traditional Chinese thought. A great deal of lore on this subject is said to have been transmitted by Jiang Shang (Chiang Shang), mentor of King Wen, one of the founders of the Zhou (Chou) dynasty. King Wen was among the culture heroes honored by Confucius and is believed to be one of the authors of the Zhou *Book of Change.*

BOOK OF CHANGE 7

Although Confucius himself brought education to a wide range of people, in the hands of later state Confucianism secular scholarship became a political tool of the elite. Some Neo-Confucians later revived the grass-roots element of the ancient Way, fifteen to twenty centuries after the death of Confucius himself.

Analects 5:22
Confucius was in Chu sometime during his extensive travels in his late fifties and sixties.

BOOK OF CHANGE 8

This is originally a model of a feudal empire, in which territory is parceled out among local lords. Abstracted into the idea of distribution of power, in more modern terms it also fits the model of a confederacy or a democratic union, in which local and central powers cooperate based on mutual understanding of their interdependent needs and circumstances.

BOOK OF CHANGE 9

The beautification of cultured qualities is not for personal vanity but for the enhancement of the quality and value of human interaction.

Zichan (Tzu-ch'an) died in 522 B.C., when Confucius was only about thirty-two years old.

Analects 3:15

In ancient China, ritual and government were closely related, as the head of state was also the master of ceremonies for the national cult, responsible for enacting the most important rites propitiating God as the supreme ancestor of all the people.

BOOK OF CHANGE 10

Confucius distinguished between higher and lower human aims, and his ability to keep these priorities in order undoubtedly helped him through the many difficulties he encountered in his life and work.

Analects 1:15

The pupil in this story was Zigeng (Tzu-keng), one of the well-known disciples. Thirty-one years younger than Confucius, he was noted for skill in language and speech.

BOOK OF CHANGE 11

In ancient times, leadership was conceived of in terms of mediation between the divine and natural orders and the human world. From time to time in history, projects such as public conservation works, land redistribution, and price stabilization programs were undertaken as means of assisting the balance of nature and humanity, a balance thought of in its perfect state as inherently divine.

Analects 8:19, 8:21

Yao and Yü were ancient leaders traditionally idealized by Confucian political philosophers. Yao is particularly famous for having handed on the throne to someone not of his family, solely on account of merit. Yü, who inherited the throne from Yao's successor Shun, is especially known for having personally directed and participated in massive water control projects that are supposed to have saved China from a catastrophic flood in the third millennium B.C.

Analects 13:15

This was Duke Ding (Ting), ruler of Lu. Ding was in office for fifteen years, between the time Confucius was forty-four years old and the time he was fifty-nine. It is said that Confucius was consulted by Duke Ding before the teacher left Lu for an extended period of time at the age of fifty-six.

Analects 20:4

This pupil was Zizhang (Tzu-chang). One of the youngest of the noted disciples, Zizhang was nearly fifty years younger than the teacher.

BOOK OF CHANGE 12

Power is one of the things Confucius is reported to have spoken of but rarely. Nevertheless, he was unambiguous in repudiating the power of personal materialistic desires as unworthy motivation for responsible members of society.

Analects 8:18

Shun and Yao were idealized leaders of the third millennium B.C. The idea of ruling without getting involved means impersonal and impartial leadership, an ideal commonly espoused by Taoist political thinkers.

Analects 8:12

Later Neo-Confucians also complained about scholars who studied to get ahead in the world rather than to improve themselves and make themselves useful to society and worthy of advancement.

BOOK OF CHANGE 13

The famous psychologist Carl G. Jung was among those Western intellectuals who, while professing to admire the Chinese mind, believed it was not inclined to analytic thinking. Categories of analysis used in Chinese thought may not coincide with those used in Western thinking, but they are not altogether different either. There are in fact many systems of analogy and analysis used in the broad spectrum of Chinese thought.

BOOK OF CHANGE 14

Confucius and his great apostle Mencius (ca. 372–289 B.C.) believed that good was natural in humans and evil artificial.

Analects 4:5

Confucius did not consider people's hereditary circumstances so much as what they did under given conditions. He did not regard people's successes so much as what they did to achieve them.

Analects 6:28

Nanzi (Nan-tzu) was the wife of Lord Ling of the state of Wei. She had a reputation for improper behavior. The objector was Zilu, a major disciple known for his political acumen. Confucius suggests that appearances and reality may not exactly coincide, and that God is a truer judge than man. In later Confucian societies, especially that of Japan, where the principles of the Confucian teachings were identified with the policies, interests, and images of the ruling order rather than with the individual search for meaning, questions of social opinion and face could override abstract beliefs.

Top-heavy bureaucracies staffed by cliques from among privileged elites ruthlessly exploiting impoverished peasants were not the stuff of Confucius' vision of rational government. An ideally balanced individual or an ideally balanced social structure include in them the means of monitoring and correcting imbalance.

Analects 17:8

To Confucius, learning was not an attainment in itself but a means of shaping and perfecting the inherent qualities and positive potentiality of the individual.

Analects 3:22

The statesman with the three homes and families was Guan Zhong, an outstanding political scientist of the seventh century B.C. who promoted powerful and effective methods of strengthening a state. His assumption of a lifestyle comparable to that of the ruler he served represented to Confucius an example of disintegration of the social order, which would ultimately lead to an unbridled scramble for power among the lords of the ancient states. This is just what happened after Confucius' death.

BOOK OF CHANGE 16

Music had a sacred function in ancient Chinese society, and the deterioration of this function in music was one of the educational and cultural concerns of Confucius. The influence of music on the human mind has been a subject of interest in China for thousands of years, especially among Taoists.

BOOK OF CHANGE 17

Although it could be said that Confucius was working to spread education and also broaden the participation of educated people in the processes of government, he did not teach or pursue perennial sociopolitical activism. When the Way was in eclipse, Confucius considered retirement to private life a legitimate response to hardened despotism.

Analects 17:19

This selection was a favorite among Chan Buddhists, who used it to allude to an unspoken teaching going on in the midst of everyday life processes.

Analects 7:10

The foremost disciple of Confucius was Yan Hui (Yen Hui). He was very poor and died young, during the lifetime of Confucius. This saying about activity and concealment as equally valid alternatives under the right circumstances shows one way in which the teaching of Confucius was not opposed to that of Taoist ancients.

Analects 2:16

This is the classic Confucian statement of the dangers in occultism.

Analects 5:13

It is a commonplace that Confucius spoke mainly of social issues and did not deal much with abstract philosophy except in relation to concrete human problems. Taoists who claim Confucius as one of their own assert that passages like this one do not mean that Confucius did not know or teach anything on matters of great metaphysical profundity, only that he did not speak much about them openly. The rationale for this is that his society was corrupt, and he believed it impossible to deal with higher matters before first taking care of mundane affairs.

BOOK OF CHANGE 18

In later Confucian societies, various attempts were made to confer recognition and reward upon people for classical virtues, to encourage exemplary conduct among the general populace.

Analects 12:18

Having once been chief of the constabulary of Lu, Confucius had personal experience with the problems of crime and punishment. Here he expresses the view that crime among the lower classes reflects corruption in the upper classes. Ideas like this did not endear him to the despots of his time.

Analects 17:6

These instructions were given to Zizhang (Tzu-chang), one of the youngest of the noted disciples, who could not have been more than twenty years old at the time he received this lesson from the teacher.

BOOK OF CHANGE 19

Education and thought were means by which Confucius proposed that people might develop their capacities to master themselves and be of service to others.

Analects 15:3

This passage, particularly the last line about penetrating things by their underlying unity, was a favorite among Chan Buddhists and Taoists of the unitarian Complete Reality school, as well as Neo-Confucians of the so-called schools of inner design.

Analects 2:16

This passage stands out as a classic aphorism of Confucian educational philosophy. In the experience of Confucius, study was not just book learning but also reflection and practical exercise.

Although this was not observed in institutionalized Confucianism, ancient educational philosophy dating from before the time of the separation of Confucianism and Taoism did not propose the imposition of a uniform system but favored adaptation of essential knowledge to local conditions and needs.

Analects 2:9

This refers again to Yan Hui.

Analects 7:8

This passage is often quoted in Chan Buddhist literature to illustrate the importance of the effort of the learning in the total process of learning and self-transformation.

Analects 6:21

This passage offers another glimpse of what lay behind the reputed reticence of Confucius on metaphysical or spiritual subjects.

BOOK OF CHANGE 21

Although Confucius preferred moral to legal mechanisms of restraint, later Confucians imbibed Legalist doctrines and began to advocate rule by law.

Analects 14:8

Love and duty are inseparable in classical Confucian thinking.

Analects 13:6

Here is another indication of Confucius' belief that law could be effective only if rulers themselves obeyed the law and personally provided appropriate examples of behavior.

In the Chinese language and philosophies, the word *public* is connected with the idea of being impersonal, impartial, and fair.

Analects 2:21

Individual behavior, at home and in society, was considered to be on a continuum with the business of government and preservation of social order.

Analects 8:14

This passage has been interpreted as a rationale for the concentration of power in the hands of an established elite, but that view contradicts the whole thrust of Confucius' mission as an educator. An interpretation more consistent with the ideals of Confucius is that one cannot know just what is involved in discharging a responsibility until one actually has the experience. It can also be taken as a simple description of the operation of a hierarchical organization.

Analects 2:20

Here can be seen Confucius' notion of social uplift through opportunity and encouragement.

Analects 12:14

To dwell on government tirelessly and carry it out faithfully means to work for government in the interest of public service, not for personal advantage or aggrandizement.

Analects 13:2

Locating talented and worthy people for public office was something that Confucius believed should be made a prime concern of rulers. The civil service examination systems later set up in China were theoretically supposed to serve this purpose.

BOOK OF CHANGE 23

Reciprocity is central to the Confucian view of social dynamics. Confucius extolled reciprocity as "one word that can be put into practice throughout your life."

Analects 6:5

Confucius was chief of the constabulary of Lu at this time.

Analects 7:26

This passage is taken to reflect the virtues of compassion and mercy, and also modesty and frugality.

BOOK OF CHANGE 24

Inaccessibility, withdrawal, and quietude are classical techniques of psychological and physical preservation, particularly recommended in times of extremes in the weather or in the course of human events.

Analects 14:1

Confucius was not just an activist; he also advocated judicious withdrawal from public affairs under certain circumstances.

Analects 15:17

Confucius regarded self-development as a necessary basis for public service. The classical Confucian response to situations in which no positive action is possible at a given moment is to turn inward to build up character and strength.

BOOK OF CHANGE 25

The ancient kings and their courts were supposed to watch over the seasonal activities of the people and assist the orderly accomplishment of the yearly cycle of production. The ancient courts' patronage of conservation and public welfare was regarded as evidence of its fitness for the divine mandate to govern.

Analects 6:30

The disciple was Zigeng. This passage is one of the clearest utterances of Confucius on the subject of humaneness.

Analects 13:9

Although Confucius thought a materialistic outlook on life to be petty and confusing, he nevertheless recognized the material element in social welfare and order. His later apostle Mencius, who wrote during the era of the Warring States, was even more explicit on this point.

BOOK OF CHANGE 26

Confucius believed that by studying history people could tune their intellectual and ethical sensibilities, heightening their awareness of cause-and-effect relationships in human affairs. This in turn could prepare them for roles of responsibility and leadership in society at all levels.

Analects 7:16

One way of reading this passage does not mention the *Book of Change,* but has Confucius say that he could be free of major errors when he had studied for fifty years. Another interpretation reads "fifty years" as referring to age, having Confucius study the *Book of Change* from the age of fifty. There is also a myth that Confucius did not start studying the book until he was seventy, supposedly because of its great profundity. The version that substitutes a different character in place of that for *change* is favored by scholars who doubt the existence of the *Book of Change* in the time of Confucius. The version that has Confucius reading the book in old age is favored by those who tend to look upon the *Book of Change* as obscure and somehow distant from the other Chinese classics. My view is that there are no grounds for assuming the book did not exist and no reason for supposing that Confucius did not pursue the knowledge expounded in this classic as avidly as he did the knowledge expounded in the other classics. At some point he apparently realized he was going to have to live longer than he might reasonably expect to in order to be able to study the *Book of Change* for the fifty years he found it would require to master to the degree of freedom from major errors. According to his own statement, at the age of seventy Confucius could do what he wanted without going over the line, and it is not at all unlikely that he began to study the *Book of Change* at the age of twenty, when by his own account he would have already spent five years at serious study of classical literature. It is also not unlikely that this statement of Confucius about the *Book of Change* in his own life was not made for autobiographical purposes but for the edification and admonition of students. See also *Analects* 3:15 in this same group of selections.

Analects 7:27

To "hear a lot" means to "learn a lot." The verb for hearing is classically used because of the importance of oral tradition, but it also came to apply to reading and research or to the whole process of information gathering.

Analects 3:15

The succession of the Xia (Hsia), Yin, and Zhou (Chou) cultures is represented by the three books of change: the *Lianshan Yi (Lien-shan I)* or *Linked Mountain Changes* of the Xia, the *Guizang Yi (Kuei-tsang I)* or *Ultimate Storehouse Changes* of the Yin, and the *Zhou Yi (Chou I)* or *Universal Changes* of the Zhou. These ancient books are believed to hold the foundation of ideas underlying each of those societies. Only the last book survives today, the *Universal Changes of the Zhou,* which is the perennially popular *Book of Change.*

BOOK OF CHANGE 27

Watchfulness and moderation, both when alone and in company, are watchwords of day-to-day Confucian practice of self-cultivation.

Analects 7:20

This passage is often cited as a classic illustration of the practical bent of Confucius.

Analects 9:1

Confucius regarded profit as a source of disorder. He seems to have regarded fate as imponderable except in terms of the evident or discoverable requirements of life. Though humaneness is mentioned many times in the *Analects* and is regarded as a cornerstone of Confucian teaching, Confucius seemed reluctant to define it too rigidly or narrowly. In 12:4 Confucius seems to say the difficulty of humaneness is a reason to speak of it rarely.

BOOK OF CHANGE 28

In order to maintain a moral stand in a time and place marked by corruption, people need the psychological fortitude to endure ostracism and isolation. If they can be manipulated by peer pressure or public opinion, they cannot be objective in their attitudes and cannot see beyond the temporary mentality of the moment. All the passages from the *Analects* quoted here relate to individual moral independence; this is where Confucius, whose teaching is called the Soft Way, comes closest to ferocity.

In Confucianism, a scholar-teacher was almost like a priest in other religions, in the sense that the ideal was an inner transformation that would develop an exemplary character and enable the individual to help others to achieve their own self-improvement.

Analects 4:18

The task of teaching, as a function of society, is not only that of the elder generation teaching the younger generation, but also that of the younger generation teaching the older generation, according to the changes in the times. Nevertheless, even though the inevitability of change was well recognized in Chinese philosophy, the admonition of the older generation by the younger generation was considered a delicate matter, since the younger owed the elder their lives.

Analects 15:16

The effort of the student, rightly oriented, is regarded as an indispensable ingredient in classical Confucian, Buddhist, and Taoist systems of learning. The teacher cannot hand out wisdom but can only help others learn how to seek personal experience of wisdom themselves.

BOOK OF CHANGE 30

The great figures of the Confucian worldview are the founders of civilization and culture, who established instruments useful to the community at large.

Analects 3:24

Confucius did not have the prestige in his own time that his name would command later on in history, but the political unrest and intellectual ferment of the age of Confucius indicate the existence of a widespread and growing desire for renewal of the civilization and its cultural ideals.

BOOK OF CHANGE 31

The original Confucian method of enlarging a state was to provide security and opportunity and thus to attract allegiance by offering expanded possibilities for participation in the benefits of society. On the level of personal conduct, this Confucian principle means to be demanding with oneself and magnanimous toward others.

BOOK OF CHANGE 32

Confucius said of himself that he had attained an unwavering state of mind when he was forty. His idea of responsibility meant standing firmly on principle and not compromising for personal advantage.

Analects 1:11

Three years was the customary period of mourning for one's father. In patriarchal Chinese society, a man was not ordinarily fully mature as an individual social entity until he had mourned his father.

Analects 4:8

Chan Buddhists cite this passage to illustrate single-minded concentration on the Way and also the transcendental completeness of the Way.

BOOK OF CHANGE 33

Human associations are a primary source of learning and character development; choices made with this in mind do not necessarily reflect personal emotions.

Analects 13:21

Centered balance is a cardinal virtue repeatedly extolled in the classic *Book of Change.*

Analects 13:25

Two points are illustrated here. One is that principle should be placed above personality. The second is that people should be engaged in work for which they are suited.

Analects 13:24

From this point of view, someone who is liked by everyone may be suspected of being a hypocrite who curries favor with everyone. A Chinese proverb says, "Truthful words offend the ears," so it is regarded as commonplace for people who speak truthfully to be resented.

BOOK OF CHANGE 34

Commenting on this image, the famous Neo-Confucian Zhu Xi (Chu Hsi) quotes the Taoist classic *Tao Te Ching:* "Those who conquer themselves are strong."

Analects 5:12

This is generally taken as a statement of the Golden Rule. Viewed in another way, it can mean that if you are unable to bear hearing others tell the truth, you will be reluctant to tell the truth to others.

Analects 6:14

This disciple was Ziyou (Tzu-yu), who was forty-five years younger than Confucius. One of the noted pupils, Ziyou was said to be outstanding in literary studies.

BOOK OF CHANGE 35

Ideal Confucian rulers are supposed to be exemplary people

themselves, personally illustrating the virtue and wisdom to validate their leadership.

Analects 14:29

Contrast this with the meaning of the modern American expression "politician's promise."

Analects 14:44

Seriousness was made a fundamental watchword by Neo-Confucians fifteen centuries after Confucius. They used the term to refer to single-minded attention.

BOOK OF CHANGE 36

Communication among the different strata of society was considered essential for tranquillity by Confucian and Taoist philosophers and tacticians following the tradition of the *Book of Change.* The image of individuals with exceptional knowledge or wisdom living inconspicuously among the people is very old in Chinese history and legend; Confucius and other advanced intellectuals derived a lot of their sociological concern from their personal familiarity with the lot of the common folk.

Analects 8:1

Uncle Tai was the elder brother of the father of King Wen of Zhou (Chou). He left the state to allow for the undisputed succession of his younger brother, in the interests of the eventual enthronement of the younger brother's exceptional son, the future King Wen.

BOOK OF CHANGE 37

The quality of trustworthiness is one of the cardinal Confucian virtues.

Analects 4:15

The saying of Confucius that his Way was permeated by unity was a favorite of Buddhists and Taoists. We are not told whether Confucius agreed with his disciple's definition of the unifying principle of the Way. The disciple was Master Zeng (Tseng), one of the most distinguished pupils.

Analects 5:5

Other distinguished philosophers like Lao-tzu and Mo-tzu wrote about the corrupting influence of professional rhetoricians.

Analects 14:23

Loyalty does not mean, as commonly assumed, simply obedience and conformity; a loyal minister is one who tells the truth, or gives sincere advice, even at the risk of angering a ruler. The disciple in this passage was Zilu (Tzu-lu), who was only nine years younger than Confucius. Zilu had been a kind of vigilante or knight-errant before meeting Confucius and becoming converted to the way of the educator. Zilu was particularly noted for his acumen in political and administrative affairs.

Analects 18:2

The man was Liangxia (Liang-hsia) Hui, a grandee of Lu famed in tradition as a man of exemplary integrity.

BOOK OF CHANGE 38

Confucius distinguished socially necessary cooperation and harmony from automatic conformism.

Analects 7:21

Gautama Buddha, a great contemporary of Confucius, is reported to have admonished people to choose their moral betters for companions.

People of the ancient Yin dynasty were inclined to believe in God and spirits outside of themselves; the thought of the succeeding Zhou (Chou) dynasty was oriented more toward the idea of resonance between the sacred outside the self and the sacred within the self. As a monument of intellectual history, the Zhou *Book of Change* is particularly significant in its representation of a shift in emphasis from divination to introspection.

Analects 7:5

The Duke of Zhou was a son of King Wen and a distinguished administrator of the early Zhou (Chou) dynasty government. Taoism still retains an ancient practice using mental images of historical or legendary figures as focal points for contemplation based on specific ideas or attributes those figures represent.

Punishments in ancient China were notoriously harsh and cruel, often consisting of physical maiming. Many social philosophers, particularly Taoists and Confucian purists, advocated reduction and minimization of penalties, along with more direct attention to the roots of crime.

Analects 2:3

Confucius seems to have always believed that external political and social reforms could only become lasting realities through inner personal reform.

Analects 5:23

Bo Yi (Po I) and Shu Qi (Shu Ch'i) were scions of a noble house who lived in the last days of the Yin dynasty. They deferred inheritance of their father's domain to each other, then left their holdings altogether and went into the mountains when the Yin dynasty finally collapsed in the final decades of the twelfth century B.C. The brothers died of starvation in the mountains. They are famous in tradition as moral purists.

BOOK OF CHANGE 41

Chinese Buddhist tradition also counts wrath and cupidity as commonplace psychological toxins that poison the mind and character. Chinese translation of the term *wrath*, which in Indian tradition was actually hatred or hostility, was undoubtedly influenced by this classic Chinese proverb from the *Book of Change*.

Analects 14:11

It is not easy to assess the material lot of Yin dynasty slaves or Zhou dynasty serfs, but it would seem logical that chronic poverty had not in the time of Confucius yet assumed the dimensions it would reach during and after the era of the Warring States, which began around the time Confucius died and lasted for more than two hundred years.

Analects 17:15

Chan Buddhists also made much of the observation that a more objective perspective on matters can be had when questions of personal gain and loss are set at a distance.

BOOK OF CHANGE 42

There is a parallel proverb from the main body of the *Book of Change*, "working hard all day, cautious at night," commonly used in Taoism to refer to this process of self-cultivation by eliminating faults and fostering virtues.

Analects 6:3

The disciple was the great Yan Hui.

Analects 15:30

The great eleventh-century Chan Master Yuanwu said, "Since time immemorial, all have lauded the ability to correct faults as being wise, rather than considering having no faults to be beautiful."

Analects 7:29

There are at least two meanings herein yielding statements of great significance: humaneness is in the very desire to be humane; and sincerity (in this case genuine desire for humaneness) is the key to making principles effective realities in practice.

BOOK OF CHANGE 43

As in Buddhism, the ideal of giving in pristine Confucianism precludes self-congratulation or expectation of gratitude or other reward.

BOOK OF CHANGE 44

The Confucian idea of rulership involved articulation of informed policies that would accord with the needs and resources of the people at large and thereby win their support.

BOOK OF CHANGE 45

In the classical political philosophies of Confucianism and Taoism, armament and military action were supposed to be for defensive purposes and not for territorial expansion. Combat and armament are also used in philosophical texts to symbolize all manner of internal and external struggle and conflict.

Analects 15:1

Confucius probably had in fact learned something about military affairs, given his background and the times in which he lived. What he wanted to emphasize, however, was the overwhelming importance of the cultural and pacifistic nature of his educational mission, not his personal acumen in matters of tactics and strategy, which were studied and professed by many men of his class.

BOOK OF CHANGE 46

Many of the subtler aspects of Confucianism are in everyday affairs. It is not necessary to always associate development of virtue with grandiose works, when there are always opportunities to develop character in the course of ordinary interactions and undertakings.

Analects 12:1

There was an elaborate body of ritual governing behavior in Zhou society, but much of it dealt with special occasions. The general idea of ritual was both expressive and didactic, using the commemoration of certain fundamental ideas, as well as the moderating and civilizing influence of exposure to courtesy in everyday life, as tools for the training of personality and character. For specialists like Confucius, study of the origins and original meanings of ancient ritual had an even deeper significance for their clues to certain psychological bases of human civilization.

Analects 5:9

To understand ten things when one thing is learned came to be a traditional description of acuity.

Analects 11:20

Like Taoism and Buddhism, Confucianism values practical application rather than mere theoretical philosophy.

Analects 13:17

The disciple was Zixia (Tzu-hsia). Forty-four years younger than Confucius, he was distinguished in literary studies.

Analects 14:37

The idea of a direct relationship to God through individual conscience gave Confucius a degree of moral fortitude that his social and political milieu could not have otherwise supported.

BOOK OF CHANGE 47

According to *Huainanzi (Huai-nan-tzu),* a Taoist-Confucian text of the second century B.C., in an enlightened social order all things and all beings find their places, so that there are no wasted people and no wasted things.

Analects 5:26

The first disciple to speak was Zilu; the second was Yan Hui, the foremost pupil of Confucius.

Analects 5:2

The disciple was Nan Rong (Nan Jung), or Nan-gong Zirong (Nan-kung Tzu-jung). He is noted elsewhere in the *Analects* for going over and over a classic verse that says, "Flaws in a white jade can still be polished off, but flaws in speech cannot be amended."

Analects 15:31

Elsewhere Confucius speaks of the complementarity of study and thought.

BOOK OF CHANGE 48

Confucius believed that hereditary status was not a sufficient basis for leadership and that the upper classes had a moral obligation to look after the needs of the people.

Analects 5:17

The man was Yan Ying (Yen Ying), a distinguished prime minister of the state of Qi, an older contemporary of Confucius.

Analects 12:7

In some sense, the material basis of society is fundamental, but the securing of the material basis itself depends on cooperative human effort.

BOOK OF CHANGE 49

Definition and prediction of climate and weather patterns was one of the most important tasks in an agrarian culture. The ancient Chinese Taoists devised a very elaborate and precise system of defining gradual changes in weather over the course of a year, along with specific strategies for human adaptation to those changes. Metaphorically, the calendar also refers to the vicissitudes of political, social, and psychological climates, as well as to the stages of human life.

BOOK OF CHANGE 50

Insofar as human beings are social animals, their individual and collective well-being depends on each member of society's finding a useful place in the community structure.

Analects 9:29

This saying is often cited in Chan Buddhist literature. On one level it means that hardship can bring out the best in people; or that difficulty brings out people's true characters, so that they can be seen for what they really are. In Chan it also means that the essence of the mind remains intact after the dross of temporal conditioning has been removed.

BOOK OF CHANGE 51

The proverbial maxim used by Confucians, Taoists, and Buddhists alike is "seek it in yourself." For Confucius, introspection was part of the mechanism of self-correction, a way to clarify the inner link of the individual conscience to the will of God.

Analects 9:4

This passage is a favorite among Chan Buddhists, whose teaching it resembles.

Analects 5:6

Confucius was pleased because his pupil was more concerned about his ability to perform a job well than about his opportunity to obtain the job.

BOOK OF CHANGE 52

Thought that is grounded in practical realities must be relevant to the circumstances and capacities of the individual concerned.

Analects 13:22

The occupations of shaman and physician demand special concentration and dedication. The implication is that even such specialities demand constancy; therefore, to achieve a comprehensive development of the whole person must require (at least) as much devotion as it takes to become a shaman or a physician.

BOOK OF CHANGE 53

Taoists were particularly keen on the idea of unspoken guidance whereby the customs and mores of a people could be elevated by the charisma of developed individuals living among them.

Analects 6:13

Taoists and Chan Buddhists were particularly emphatic in declaring trivial pedantry a perversion of education. Their criticisms of later Confucian academicians were often based on the charge that they had the appearance of learning but had lost the reality. The rise of Neo-Confucianism fifteen hundred years after Confucius was due in part to an attempt to correct this decadence.

BOOK OF CHANGE 54

One of the didactic techniques of Confucius was to analyze elements of character, personality, and performance in order to observe their effect in combination and find out where there might be any imbalance.

BOOK OF CHANGE 55

Although Confucius was not confident of the efficacy of punishment in the development of inner character, the state of society in his time was such that it obviously could not dispense with formal mechanisms of law and order. Confucius himself had experience in the criminal justice system of his native state of Lu. Short of the inner reform of the mind of society that would make penal codes unnecessary, philosophers like Confucius were concerned that legal judgments be made fairly and impartially, not influenced by the personal biases of people in positions of authority.

BOOK OF CHANGE 56

In ancient Chinese metaphor, humaneness and justice (bases of Confucian political teaching) are represented by spring and autumn and associated with reward and punishment. The metaphor of natural cycles reinforced the concept that these two aspects of polity should be practiced in a balanced and timely manner.

Analects 4:2

If the inhumane live in austerity too long, they become morbid and cruel; if they live in comfort too long, they become arrogant and capricious.

Later Taoist alchemists, who absorbed certain ideas of Confucius into their own practice, believed that spiritual states attained by inner contemplative exercises had to be stabilized by good works in the human world order to become permanent.

Analects 3:19

Courtesy on the part of people in positions of authority toward their subordinates might seem trivial to a purely materialistic cost-benefit analysis, but it is nevertheless of importance in maintaining organizational cohesion and therefore efficiency.

Analects 4:17

There is a play on words here; the words for government (*zheng/cheng*) and rectitude (*zheng/cheng*) are written similarly and pronounced the same.

BOOK OF CHANGE 58

Even though his school was private in the sense of being independent of government institutions, Confucius may be said to have been a pioneer in the spirit of public education in that he worked to make formal learning available to a wider range of people beyond the hereditary elite. Later Neo-Confucians also set up grass-roots associations for education and charitable works.

Analects 15:27

After a kind of Confucianism had been made into the official orthodoxy in the second century B.C., colleges were set up to indoctrinate the scions of the ruling class. Subsequently clan factions and cliques came to dominate the system, so that many conscientious scholars without high family connections had no real opportunity to work in government and therefore turned away from Confucian studies.

In ancient times, the king was not only a civil leader but also a religious leader, in the sense of being the chief figurehead of the national ancestral cult. As each clan honored its individual ancestors, the king honored the supreme God as the ancestor of all the people.

Analects 8:21

Yü's custom of wearing ragged clothes but beautifying ceremonial garb signifies refusal to use political power for personal gain and greater respect for the role of religious and spiritual leadership.

Analects 3:3

Evidently what Confucius really valued was not the form but the spirit of rites and music.

BOOK OF CHANGE 60

The morality of Confucius was not precisely defined by a rigid set of rules but by the principle of appropriate measure.

Analects 12:23

According to Confucius, whether in professional associations or in private society, loyalty and truthfulness go together.

BOOK OF CHANGE 61

In old Chinese penal law, people were executed not only as individuals but in families and groups. This was done to intimidate the populace and to exterminate potential enemies of the state. Early Confucians and Taoists both regarded harsh punishment as a sign of corruption in government. Having professional experience in the field, Confucius cannot but have understood the need for law and order as well as the shortcomings of the prevailing customs; he believed the real solution to social problems could not be obtained by coercion but lay in the regeneration of character.

Analects 11:19

One reason Confucius did not believe in the regenerative power of punishment was that he considered the moral quality of leadership to be the most telling influence on the mores of the people at large.

BOOK OF CHANGE 62

According to Confucian canons of behavior, cultivated people are careful to avoid excess; but if they are excessive in anything, their excess is not in self-indulgence but in the diligent performance of social niceties.

BOOK OF CHANGE 63

History and the *Book of Change* are basic sources of Confucian study because combined study of concrete events and abstract principles is valuable in the development of foresight.

Analects 6:5

The implication is that the disciple is ready to leave the country rather than serve a corrupt noble yet is also ready to return if the noble mends his own ways.

Analects 3:13

The grandee was intimating that he was more powerful than the titular head of state. Confucius replies that a warp in the sociopolitical order will inevitably produce adverse consequences. The grandee is talking about power politics; Confucius is talking about ethical politics.

Analects 8:13

This passage suggests that Confucius did not consider it a point of duty for educated people to serve in public office or take an active role in public life regardless of the conditions of the time and place.

BOOK OF CHANGE 64

One of the mottoes of Confucian learning is to "investigate things to produce knowledge." This was interpreted in various ways over the ages, however, with some Confucians falling back on fixed systems to classify things, while others emphasized the development of intellectual capacity and the extension of insight and experience.

Analects 5:8

Many philosophers considered evaluation of individual qualities and talents one of the most important tasks of rulership.

Analects 5:19

Humaneness is ordinarily considered the fundamental virtue in Confucian thinking. Here Confucius indicates that this quality is not a state of emotion but an attitude based on specific knowledge of the human condition.

Analects 5:21

"Ignorance" here refers to defensive dissimulation. Here again it seems evident that Confucius did not preach activism under all circumstances but saw disengagement as a morally authentic choice under certain conditions.

Analects 15:28

The *Tao Te Ching* conveys a similar message in saying, "When everyone knows good is good, this is not good."